CAXTON
ITALIAN
PHRASEBOOK

CAXTON EDITIONS

First published in Great Britain by
CAXTON EDITIONS
an imprint of
the Caxton Book Company Ltd
16 Connaught Street
Marble Arch
London W2 2AF

This edition copyright
© 1999 CAXTON EDITIONS

Prepared and designed
for Caxton Editions by
Superlaunch Limited
PO Box 207
Abingdon
Oxfordshire OX13 6TA

Consultant editors Simon Image
and Paola Pesavento

ISBN 1 84067 067 3

A copy of the CIP data for this book is available from
the British Library upon request

Printed and bound in India

CONTENTS

Know before you go
4

Travel
41

Accommodation
113

Banking and Shopping
135

Emergencies
169

Food and Entertainment
184

Further Information
234

Where to find
237

Pronunciation is given in *italic type* and these phonetic spellings. They are intended as a broad outline only, which will be easy to remember. We have used ***bold italics*** to show stresses, and hyphens to separate the syllables for faster reading.

Note: when a letter is doubled, each of the two letters must be sounded individually.

Vowels

a long, as in f*a*ther

e short, as in m*e*t

è open, as in *eh*? who?

i like *ee*, as in f*ee*l

o short, as in h*o*t

u like *oo*, as in c*oo*l

Dipthongs

Basically, Italians give full value to every single letter. Hence we show vowels which follow each other as separate syllables, following the scheme above:

ae = ah-eh

ai = ah-ee

au = ah-oo

eu = eh-oo

ie = ee-eh

iu = ee-oo

ou = oh-oo

uo = oo-oh

Consonants

c before *i* and *e* (ci, ce) soft *ch* as in *ch*eek
c before *a, o, u* (ca, co, cu) hard *c* as in *c*at
g before *i* and *e* (gi, ge) soft *j* as in *j*ittery,
 *j*elly, *g*in, *g*elignite
g before *a, o, u* (ga, go, gu) hard *g* as in
 *g*allon, *g*ossip, *g*uzzle
sc before *i* or *e* (sci, sce) soft *sh* as in *sh*ip,
 *sh*e
sc before *a, o, u* (sca, sco, scu) hard *sk* as in
 *sc*apular, *Sc*ottish, *sc*ullery
gli silent *g*, pronounced *ly*, as in mil*li*on
gn silent *g*, pronounced *ny*, as in
 compa*ni*on (often given as *n-y*)
qu hard *kw* sound, as in *qu*otation
z sounds as *ts* as in Zeppelin, sometimes *dz*
zz sounds as *dz* as in a*dz*e, sometimes as *t-ts*

There is not enough space to include the
word please in every request translated in
this book. However, the word can never
be used enough when requesting help.

please	**thank you**
per favore	grazie
*pehr fah-**voh**-reh*	***graht**-see-eh*

Monday, Tuesday
Lunedì, Martedì
*Loo-neh-**dee**, Mar-teh-**dee***

Wednesday, Thursday
Mercoledì, Giovedì
*Mehr-koh-leh-**dee**, Joh-veh-**dee***

Friday, Saturday, Sunday
Venerdì, Sabato, Domenica
*Veh-nehr-**dee**, **Sah**-bah-toh, Doh-**meh**-nee-kah*

public holiday
giorni festivi
***johr**-nee feh-**stee**-vee*

day off
giorno libero
***johr**-noh **lee**-beh-roh*

January, February, March
Gennaio, Febbraio, Marzo
*Jehn-**nah**-ee-oh, Fehb-**brah**-ee-oh, **Mahr**-tsoh*

April, May, June, July
Aprile, Maggio, Guigno, Luglio
*Ahp-**ree**-leh, **Maj**-joh, **Joon**-yoh, **Lool**-yoh*

August, September, October
Agosto, Settembre, Ottobre
*Ah-**goh**-stoh, Set-**tem**-breh, Ot-**toh**-breh*

November, December
Novembre, Dicembre
*Noh-**vem**-breh, Dee-**chem**-breh*

today, tomorrow (afternoon)
oggi, domani (pomeriggio)
***oj**-jee, doh-**mahn**-ee (poh-meh-**reej**-joh)*

yesterday (morning)
ieri (mattina)
*ee-**eh**-ree (mat-**tee**-nah)*

tonight
stasera / stanotte
*stah-**seh**-rah / stah-**not**-teh*

(next) week
(la prossima) settimana
*(lah **pros**-see-mah) seht-tee-**mah**-nah*

(last) month, a year ago
il mese (scorso), un anno fa
*eel **meh**-zeh (**skohr**-soh), oon **an**-noh **fah***

first, second, third, fourth
primo, secondo, terzo, quarto
pree-moh, seh-kohn-doh, tehr-tsoh, kwahr-toh

fifth, sixth, seventh, eighth
quinto, sesto, settimo, ottavo
kween-toh, seh-stoh, seh-tee-moh, oh-tah-voh

ninth, tenth, eleventh
nono, decimo, undicesimo
noh-noh, deh-cee-moh, oon-deh-cheh-see-moh

twelfth, thirteenth
dodicesimo, tredicesimo
doh-deh-cheh-see-moh, treh-dee-che-see-moh

fourteenth, fifteenth
quattordicesimo, quindicesimo
kwah-tohr-dee-che-see-moh, kween-dee-che-see-moh

sixteenth, seventeenth
sedicesimo, diciasettesimo
seh-dee-che-see-moh, dee-cha-seh-teh-see-moh

eighteenth, nineteenth
diciottesimo, diciannovesimo
dee-cho-teh-see-moh, dee-cha-noh-veh-see-moh

twentieth, twenty-first
ventesimo, ventunesimo
*vehn-**teh**-see-moh, vehn-toon-**eh**-see-moh*

twenty-second, twenty-third
ventiduesimo, ventitreesimo
*vehn-tee-doo-**eh**-see-moh, vehn-tee-treh-**eh**-see-moh*

twenty-fourth
ventiquattresimo
*vehn-tee-kwah-**treh**-see-moh*

twenty-fifth
venticinquesimo
*vehn-tee-cheen-**kweh**-see-moh*

twenty-sixth, twenty-seventh
ventiseiesimo, ventisettesimo
vehn-tee-seh-ee-eh-see-moh, vehn-tee-seh-teh-see-moh

twenty-eighth, twenty-ninth
ventottesimo, ventinovesimo
*vehn-toh-**teh**-see-moh, vehn-tee-noh-**veh**-see-moh*

thirtieth, thirty-first
trentesimo, trentunesimo
*trehn-**teh**-see-moh, trehn-toon-**eh**-see-moh*

Christmas
Natale
*nah-**tah**-leh*

Christmas holidays
Le vacanze di Natale
*leh vah-**kahn**-tseh dee nah-**tah**-leh*

Christmas Eve
La Vigilia di Natale
*lah vee-**jee**-lee-ah dee nah-**tah**-leh*

Christmas Day, 25 December
Il Giorno di Natale
*eel **johr**-noh dee nah-**tah**-leh*

Boxing Day, 26 December, St Stephen's Day
Santo Stefano
***sahn**-toh **steh**-fah-noh*

New Year's Eve
L'Ultimo dell'Anno
(San Silvestro)
***lool**-tee-moh dehl-**lahn**-noh*
*(sahn seel-**veh**-stroh)*

New Year's Day
Capodanno
(Il Primo dell'Anno)
*kah-poh-**dahn**-noh*
*(eel **pree**-moh dehl-**lahn**-noh)*

Easter
Pasqua
***pah**-skwah*

Easter Holidays
Le vacanze di Pasqua
*leh vah-**kahn**-tseh dee **pah**-skwah*

Good Friday
Venerdì Santo
*veh-nehr-**dee sahn**-toh*

Easter Eve
La Vigilia di Pasqua
*lah vee-**jee**-lee-ah dee **pah**-skwah*

Easter Day
Il Giorno di Pasqua
*eel **johr**-noh dee **pah**-skwah*

Easter Sunday
La Domenica di Pasqua
*lah Doh-**meh**-nee-kah dee **pah**-skwah*

Easter Monday
Pasquetta
*pah-**skweht**-tah*

Ferragosto
(15 August: on this day all Italy stops
completely)
Ferragosto
*fehr-rah-**goh**-stoh*

Ferragosto Holidays
(1–15 August: Italy's national holiday
period)
Le ferie di Ferragosto
(sotto ferragosto)
*leh **feh**-ree-eh dee fehr-rah-**goh**-stoh*
*(**soht**-toh fehr-rah-**goh**-stoh)*

All Saints (1 November), the day after
Halloween
Ognissanti
*ohn-yees-**sahn**-tee*

excuse me / pardon me / I'm sorry
Mi scusi
*mee **skoo**-zee*

may I get past?
posso passare?
***pos**-soh pas-**sah**-reh*

yes, no (thank you)
sì, no (grazie)
*see, noh (**grah**-tsee-eh)*

I agree (= understand)
Sono d'accordo
***soh**-noh dahk-**kohr**-doh*

I'd like, please
Vorrei, per favore
*vohr-**reh**-ee, pehr fah-**voh**-reh*

thank you
grazie
***graht**-see-eh*

Can you help me please?
Può aiutarmi per favore?
*poo-oh ah-ee-oo-tahr-mee, pehr fah-**voh**-reh*

I don't understand
Non capisco.
nohn kah-**pee**-skoh

Not at all, you're welcome (after thanks)
Di niente, prego
*dee nee-**ehn**-teh,* **preh**-goh

It's nothing / doesn't matter
Non fa niente
*nohn fah nee-**ehn**-teh*

Is it possible to ...? (= may I) **have**
Potrei avere ...?
*poh-**treh**-ee ah-**veh**-reh ...*

OK that's good, that's beautiful
Benissimo; ottimo
*beh-**nee**-see-moh;* **oht**-tee-moh

many thanks
molte grazie
***mohl**-teh* **graht**-see-eh

Is everything all right?
Va tutto bene?
***vah too**-toh* **beh**-neh

At what time is ...?
A che ora è ...?
ah keh oh-rah eh ...

... the train for ..., the bus for ...
... il treno per ..., l'autobus per ...
eel treh-noh pehr ..., lah-oo-toh-boos pehr ...

too (early), late
troppo presto, tardi
trohp-poh preh-stoh, tahr-dee

something earlier
un po' prima
oon poh pree-mah

something later
un po' più tardi
oon poh pee-oo tahr-dee

I'd like to change ...
Vorrei modificare ...
vohr-reh-ee moh-dee-fee-kah-reh ...

... the time of my booking
... la mia prenotazione
... lah mee-ah preh-noh-taht-see-oh-neh

good enough / that's fine
va bene cosí
*vah **beh**-neh koh-**zee***

public holiday
giorno festivo
***johr**-noh feh-s**tee**-voh*

Saturday, Sunday
Sabato, Domenica
***sah**-bah-toh, doh-**meh**-nee-kah*

in the morning
di mattina
*dee maht-**tee**-nah*

in the afternoon
di pomeriggio
*dee poh-meh-**reej**-joh*

in the evening
di sera
*dee **seh**-rah*

please hurry
la prego, si affretti
*lah **preh**-goh, see ahf-**freht**-tee*

I'm late
sono in ritardo
*soh-noh een ree-**tahr**-doh*

At what time is ... breakfast?
A che ora è la colazione?
*ah keh **oh**-rah **eh lah** coh-lah-tsee-**oh**-neh*

... lunch, dinner
... il pranzo, la cena
*... eel **prahn**-tsoh, lah **cheh**-nah*

At what time does it ...?
A che ora ...?
*ah keh **oh**-rah ...*

... start, finish
... comincia, finire
*... koh-**meen**-chah, fee-**nee**-reh*

open, closed
aperto, chiuso
*ah-**pehr**-toh, kee-**oo**-zoh*

leave, arrive
partire, arrivare
*pahr-**tee**-reh, ahr-ree-**vah**-reh*

17

It's one (o'clock)
È l'una
eh-loo-nah

It's nearly one o'clock
È quasi l'una
eh kwah-see loo-nah

It's ... two, three, four ...
Sono ... le due, le tre, le quattro ...
soh-noh leh doo-eh, leh treh, leh kwaht-troh

... five, six, seven ...
... le cinque, le sei, le sette ...
... leh cheen-kweh, leh seh-ee, leh seht-teh ...

... eight, nine, ten ...
... le otto, le nove, le dieci ...
... leh ot-toh, leh noh-veh, leh dee-eh-chee ...

... eleven, twelve ...
... le undici, le dodici ...
... leh oon-dee-chee, leh doh-dee-chee ...

... noon, midnight
... mezzogiorno, mezzanotte
... med-zoh-johr-noh, med-zah-not-teh

... minutes past *x*, ... minutes to *x*:

It's ten past one
È l'una e dieci
eh loo-na eh dee-eh-chee

It's twenty past two
Sono le due e venti
soh-noh leh doo-eh eh vehn-tee

It's ten to one
È l'una meno dieci
eh loo-nah meh-noh dee-eh-chee

It's twenty to two
Sono le due meno venti
soh-noh leh doo-eh meh-noh vehn-tee

a quarter to ..., (past), half-past:

It's quarter to one
È l'una meno un quarto
eh loo-nah meh-noh oon kwahr-toh

It's quarter past one
È l'una e un quarto
eh loo-nah eh oon kwahr-toh

19

It's half past one
È l'una e mezza
*eh loo-nah eh **mehd**-zah*

It's a quarter to two
Sono le due meno un quarto
*soh-noh leh **doo**-eh **meh**-noh oon **kwahr**-toh*

It's a quarter past two
Sono le due e un quarto
*soh-noh leh **doo**-eh eh oon **kwahr**-toh*

It's half past two
Sono le due e mezza
*soh-noh leh **doo**-eh eh **mehd**-zah*

the hours, the minutes
le ore, i minuti
*leh **oh**-reh, ee mee-**noo**-tee*

a quarter of an hour / half an hour
un quarto d'ora / mezz'ora
*oon **kwahr**-toh **doh**-rah / mehdz-**oh**-rah*

three-quarters of an hour
tre quarti d'ora
*treh **kwahr**-tee **doh**-rah*

Good morning / Good night
Buon giorno / buona notte
bwohn johr-noh / *bwoh*-nah *noht*-teh

Good afternoon / evening (after about 3.30pm)
Buona sera
bwoh-nah *seh*-rah

Hello (informal). **My name is ...**
Ciao. Mi chiamo ...
cha-oo. *mee kee*-*ah*-moh ...

What is your name? (informal)
Come ti chiami?
koh-meh tee *kee*-*ah*-mee

What is your name? (formal)
Come si chiama?
koh-meh see *kee*-*ah*-mah

How do you do? (formal)
Piacere di conoscerla?
pee-ah-*che*-reh dee koh-*noh*-shehr-la

Pleased to meet you (informal)
Piacere di conoscerti
pee-ah-*che*-reh dee koh-*noh*-shehr-tee

How are you? (informal / formal)
Come stai? / Come sta?
koh-meh stah-ee/koh-meh stah

Very well, thanks; and you? (informal / formal)
Molto bene, grazie; e (tu) Lei?
mohl-toh beh-neh, graht-see-eh; eh (too) leh-ee

This is my (male) **colleague ...**
Questo è il mio collega ...
kweh-stoh eh eel mee-oh kohl-leh-gah ...

... my husband, my friend (male)
... mio marito, il mio amico
mee-oh mah-ree-toh, eel mee-oh ah-mee-koh

... father, son, boyfriend
... padre, figlio, ragazzo
... pah-dreh, feel-yoh, rah-gaht-soh

... my wife, my friend (female)
... mia moglie, la mia amica
... mee-ah mohl-yeh, lah mee-ah ah-mee-kah

... daughter, mother, girlfriend
... figlia, madre, ragazza
... feel-yah, mah-dreh, rah-gaht-sah

May I introduce ...? (formal)
Posso presentarle...?
pohs-soh *preh-zehn-**tahr**-leh ...

Goodbye (from most to least formal)
Addio
*ahd-**dee**-oh*
Arrivederla
*ahr-ree-veh-**dehr**-lah*
Arrivederci
*ahr-ree-veh-**dehr**-chee*
Ci vediamo
*chee veh-dee-**ah**-moh*

See you later / soon (informal)
Ci vediamo dopo / presto
*chee veh-dee-**ah**-moh **doh**-poh / **preh**-stoh*

Until next time (informal)
Arrivederci
*ahr-ree-veh-**dehr**-chee*
Alla prossima volta
***ahl**-lah **prohs**-see-mah **vohl**-tah*

Have a good holiday / Have a good trip!
Buone vacanze / Buon viaggio!
***bwoh**-neh vah-**kahn**-tseh / boo-**ohn**- vee-**ah**-joh*

How much is the entrance fee?
Quanto costa il biglietto?
kwahn-toh koh-stah eel beel-yeht-toh

Is there a reduction for ...?
C'è uno sconto per ...?
cheh oo-noh skohn-toh pehr ...

... pensioners
... i pensionati
... *ee pehn-see-oh-nah-tee*

... students, children
... gli studenti, i bambini
... *ly stoo-dehn-tee, ee bahm-bee-nee*

... disabled
... i disabili
... *ee deez-ah-bee-lee*

... groups
... i gruppi
... *ee groop-pee*

... war veterans
... i veterani di guerra
... *ee veh-teh-rah-nee dee gwehr-rah*

How much is (this)?
Quanto costa (questo / questa)?
kwahn-toh koh-stah (kweh-stoh / kweh-stah)

How much are (these)?
Quanto costano (questi)?
kwahn-toh koh-stah-noh (kweh-stee)

I'd like to pay
Vorrei pagare
vohr-reh-ee pah-gah-reh

May I have the bill, please?
Il conto, per favore?
eel kohn-toh, pehr fah-voh-reh

Is everything included?
È tutto compreso?
eh toot-toh kohm-preh-zoh

Is VAT included?
È compresa l'IVA?
eh kohm-preh-zah lee-vah

Is service included?
È compreso il servizio?
eh kohm-preh-zoh eel sehr-vee-tsee-oh

Is it possible to pay ...?
È possibile pagare ...?
*eh pohs-**see**-bee-leh pah-**gah**-reh ...*

... by this credit card?
... con la carta di credito?
*... kohn lah **kahr**-tah dee **kreh**-dee-toh*

Do you accept travellers' / Eurocheques?
Accettate traveller's / Eurocheques
*ah-cheht-**tah**-teh **trah**-veh-lehrz/eh-**oo**-roh-shehks*

I'd like a receipt, please
Vorrei la ricevuta, per favore
*vohr-**reh**-ee lah ree-cheh-**voo**-tah, pehr fah-**voh**-re*

Thank you, this is for you
Grazie, questo è per Lei
***graht**-see-eh, **kweh**-stoh **eh** pehr **leh**-ee*

I think you've made a mistake (e.g. in the bill)
Penso che ci sia un errore
***pehn**-soh keh chee **see**-ah oon ehr-**roh**-reh*

What is this amount for?
Per che cos'è questa somma?
***pehr** keh koh-**zeh** **kweh**-stah **sohm**-mah*

---

1 euro = 1936.21 lire

Euro notes and coins will circulate from 2002; meanwhile, bank transactions are available in this currency

---

100 lire, 200 lire
cento lire, duecento lire
chehn-toh lee-reh, dooeh-cehn-toh lee-reh

1.000 lire, 15.000 lire
mille lire, quindicimila lire
meel-leh lee-reh, kween-dee-chee-mee-lah lee-reh

20.000 lire
ventimila lire
vehn-tee-mee-lah lee-reh

25.000 lire
venticinquemila lire
vehn-tee-cheen-kweh-mee-lah lee-reh

30.000 lire
trentamila lire
trehn-tah-mee-lah lee-reh

35.000 lire
trentacinquemila lire
trehn-*tah*-*cheen*-*kweh*-*mee*-*lah*　　*lee*-*reh*

40.000 lire
quarantamila lire
kwah-*rahn*-*tah*-*mee*-*lah*　　*lee*-*reh*

45.000 lire
quarantacinquemila lire
kuah-*rahn*-*tah*-*cheen*-*kweh*-*mee*-*lah*　　*lee*-*reh*

50.000 lire
cinquantamila lire
cheen-*kwahn*-*tah*-*mee*-*lah*　　*lee*-*reh*

55.000 lire
cinquantacinquemila lire
cheen-*kwahn*-*tah*-*cheen*-*kweh*-*mee*-*lah*　　*lee*-*reh*

60.000 lire
sessantamila lire
sehs-*sah*-*tah*-*mee*-*lah*　　*lee*-*reh*

65.000 lire
sessantacinque mila lire
sehs-*sahn*-*tah*-*cheen*-*kweh*-*mee*-*lah*　　*lee*-*reh*

70.000 lire
settantamila lire
*seht-**tahn**-tah-**mee**-lah* **lee**-*reh*

75.000 lire
settantacinquemila lire
*seht-**tahn**-tah-**cheen**-kweh-**mee**-lah* **lee**-*reh*

80.000 lire
ottantamila lire
*oht-**tahn**-tah-**mee**-lah* **lee**-*reh*

85.000 lire
ottantacinquemila lire
*oht-**tahn**-tah-**cheen**-kweh-**mee**-lah* **lee**-*reh*

90.000 lire
novantamila lire
*noh-**vahn**-tah-**mee**-lah* **lee**-*reh*

95.000 lire
novantacinquemila lire
*noh-**vahn**-tah-**cheen**-kweh-**mee**-lah* **lee**-*reh*

100.000 lire
centomila lire
***chen**-toh-**mee**-lah* **lee**-*reh*

200.000 lire
duecentomila lire
*doo-eh-**chen**-toh-**mee**-lah   **lee**-reh*

250.000 lire
duecentocinquantamila lire
*doo-eh-**chen**-toh-cheen-**kwahn**-tah-**mee**-lah
lee-reh*

300.000 lire
trecentomila lire
*treh-**chen**-toh-**mee**-lah   **lee**-reh*

400.000 lire
quattrocentomila lire
*kwaht-troh-**chen**-toh-**mee**-lah   **lee**-reh*

500.000 lire
cinquecentomila lire /
mezzo milione di lire
*cheen-kweh-**chen**-toh-**mee**-lah   **lee**-reh /
mehd-soh mee-lee-**oh**-neh dee **lee**-reh*

600.000 lire
seicentomila lire
*seh-ee-**chen**-toh-**mee**-lah   **lee**-reh*

700.000 lire
settecentomila lire
*seht-teh-**chen**-toh-**mee**-lah*   *lee-reh*

800.000 lire
ottocentomila lire
*oht-toh-**chehn**-toh-**mee**-lah*   *lee-reh*

900.000 lire
novecentomilalire
*noh-veh-**chehn**-toh-**mee**-lah*   *lee-reh*

1.000.000 lire
un milione di lire
*oon mee-lee-**oh**-neh dee **lee**-reh*

1.500.000 lire
un milione e mezzo di lire
*oon mee-lee-**oh**-neh eh **med**-soh dee **lee**-reh*

2.000.000 lire
due milioni di lire
***doo**-eh mee-lee-**oh**-nee dee **lee**-reh*

10.000.000 lire
dieci milioni di lire
*dee-**eh**-chee mee-lee-**oh**-nee dee **lee**-reh*

I'm sorry ...
Mi dispiace ...
*mee dee-spee-**ah**-cheh* **...**

I don't speak Italian
non parlo Italiano
*nohn **pahr**-loh ee-tah-lee-**ah**-noh*

Is it possible to speak ...?
Si potrebbe parlare ...?
*see poh-**trehb**-beh pahr-**lah**-reh ...*

... in (English), please
... in (inglese), per favore
*... een een-**gleh**-seh, pehr fah-**voh**-reh*

in French, German, Spanish
in francese, tedesco, spagnolo
*een frahn-**cheh**-zeh, teh-**deh**-skoh, spahn-**yoh**-loh*

I'm sorry, I don't understand
Mi dispiace, non capisco
*mee dee-spee-**ah**-cheh, nohn kah-**pee**-skoh*

Yes, that's clear (I understand)
Sì, ho capito
***see**, oh kah-**pee**-toh*

Can you repeat that, slowly?
Potrebbe ripetere, lentamente?
poh-__trehb__-beh ree-__peh__-teh-reh, lehn-tah-__mehn__-teh

Could you write that down for me?
Potrebbe trascrivermi questo?
poh-__trehb__-beh trah-__skree__-vehr-mee __kweh__-stoh

Do you understand (what I say)?
Capisce (quello che dico)?
kah-__pee__-sheh (__kwehl__-loh keh __dee__-koh)

Just a moment, please
Un momento, prego
oon moh-__mehn__-toh, __preh__-goh

Yes, that's right
Sì, giusto / Sì, ho capito
__see__, __joo__-stoh / __see__, oh kah-__pee__-toh

How do you say ...? / What do you call ...?
Come si dice ...?
__koh__-meh see __dee__-cheh ...

I'm not sure
Non sono sicuro
nohn __soh__-noh see-__koo__-roh

To use public telephones in Italy you need either telephone tokens (gettoni telefonici) or telephone cards (schede telefoniche). These are generally bought from newspaper stands and tobacco shops. Sometimes it is also possible to use credit cards.

Excuse me, where is ...?
Mi scusi, dov'è ...?
*mee **skoo**-zee, doh-**veh** ...*

... the telephone box
... la cabina del telefono
*... lah kah-**bee**-nah dehl teh-**leh**-fohnoh*

I'd like (some) ... I would like a
Vorrei (qualche) ...Vorrei una
*vohr-**reh**-ee (**kwahl**-keh) ... vohr-**reh**-ee **oo**-nah*

... telephone token, (telephone tokens)
... gettone telefonico, (gettoni telefonici)
*jeht-**toh**-neh(nee) teh-**leh**-foh-nee-koh(kee)*

a 5000 lire telephone card, please
una scheda telefonica da
5000 (cinquemila) lire, per favore
*oo-nah **skeh**-dah teh-leh-**foh**-nee-kah dah*
*cheen-kweh-**mee**-lah **lee**-reh, pehr fah-**voh**-reh*

a 10.000 / 20.000 lire (card)
da 10000 (diecimila)
*dah dee-eh-chee-**mee**-lah*
20000 (ventimila) lire
*vehn-tee-**mee**-lah **lee**-reh*

Can I telephone ...?
Posso chiamare ...?
***pohs**-soh kee-ah-**mah**-reh ...*

... (England) from here
... (l'Inghilterra) da qui
*... (leen-geel-**tehr**-rah) dah **kwee***

Can you give me the code ...?
Potrebbe darmi il prefisso ...?
*poht-**trehb**-beh **dahr**-mee eel preh-**fees**-soh*

... (for America), please
... per l'America, per favore
*... pehr la-**meh**-ree-kah, pehr fah-**voh**-reh*

I'd like a person-to-person call
Vorrei parlare con una persona specifica,
e non dovere pagare se rispondesse
qualcun altro
*vohr-**reh**-ee pahr-**lah**-reh kohn **oo**-nah*
*pehr-**soh**-nah speh-**chee**-fee-kah, eh nohn*
*doh-**veh**-reh pah-**gah**-reh seh*
*ree-spohn-**dehs**-seh kwahl-**koon** **ahl**-troh*

I'd like a reversed-charge call, please
Vorrei fare una telefonata a carico del
ricevente, per favore
*vohr-**reh**-ee **fah**-reh oo-nah*
*teh-leh-foh-**nah**-tah ah **kah**-ree-koh **dehl**
*ree-cheh-**vehn**-teh, pehr fah-**voh**-reh*

How do I get the international operator?
Come posso parlare con il centralino
telefonate internazionali?
***koh**-meh **pohs**-soh pahr-**lah**-reh kohn eel*
*chehn-trah-**lee**-noh teh-leh-foh-**nah**-teh*
*een-tehr-nat-see-oh-**nah**-lee*

Hello, this is ... speaking
Buongiorno, sono ...
*bwohn **johr**noh, **soh**noh ...*

I'd like to speak to ...
Vorrei parlare con ...
*vohr-**reh**-ee pahr-**lah**-reh kohn ...*

Speak (louder), ... please
Parli (più forte), ... per favore
***pahr**-lee (pee-**oo fohr**-teh), ... pehr fah-**voh**-reh*

... more slowly, please
... più lentamente, per favore
*... pee-**oo** lehn-tah-**mehn**-teh, pehr fah-**voh**-reh*

I'll hold on
Aspetto in linea
*ahs-**peht**-toh een **lee**-nee-ah*

When can I call back?
Quando posso richiamare?
***kwahn**-doh **pohs**-soh ree-kee-ah-**mah**-reh*

Please will you give him (her) ...?
Potrebbe lasciargli (lasciarle) ...?
*poh-**trehb**-beh lah-**shar**-lyee (lah-**shar**-leh)*

... a message
... un messaggio
*... oon mehs-**saj**-oh*

cheh oo-na teh-leh-foh-nah-tah pehr leh-ee
C'è una telefonata per Lei
There's a phone call for you

aht-tehn-dah oon aht-tee-moh, pehr fah-voh-reh
Attenda un attimo, per favore
Hold the line

nohn cheh ree-spoh-stah
Non c'è risposta
There's no answer

lah lee-neh-ah eh ok-koo-pah-tah
La linea è occupata
The line is engaged

eel teh-leh-foh-noh nohn foon-tsee-oh-nah
Il telefono non funziona
The phone is not working

eh fwoh-ree ahl moh-mehn-toh
È fuori al momento
He (she) is out at the moment

ah zba-lee-yah-toh noo-meh-roh
Ha sbagliato numero
You have the wrong number

a as in **Ancona**, b / **Bologna**
a come Ancona, b / Bologna
ah koh-meh ahn-koh-nah, bee / boh-loh-nyah

c / **Cagliari**, d / **Domodossola**
Ci / Cagliari, Di / Domodossola
chee / kah-ly-ah-ree, dee / doh-moh-dohs-soh-lah

e as in **Emboli**, f / **Florence**
E come Empoli, effe / Firenze
eh koh-meh ehm-poh-lee, ehf-eh / fee-rehn-tseh

g as in **Genoa**, h / **Hollywood**
Gi come Genova, acca / Hollywood
jee koh-meh jeh-noh-vah, ahk-kah / Hollywood

i as in **Imola**, j / **jo-jo**
I come Imola, I lunga / jo-jo
ee koh-meh ee-moh-lah, ee loon-hah / yoh-yoh

k as in **Kenya**, l / **Livorno**
Kappa come Kenia, elle / Livorno
kahp-pah / keh-nee-ah, ehl-leh / lee-vohr-noh

m / **Mantua**, n / **Novara**
emme / Mantova, enne / Novara
ehm-meh / mahn-toh-vah, ehn-neh / noh-vah-rah

o as in Otranto, p / Pisa
O come Otranto, Pi / Pisa
oh koh-meh oh-trahn-toh, pee / pee-sah

q as in Quadro, r / Rome
Qu come Quadro, erre / Roma
koo koh-meh kwah-droh, ehr-reh / roh-mah

s as in Savona, t / Trapani
esse come Savona, t / Trapani
ehs-seh koh-meh sah-voh-nah, tee/trah-pah-nee

u as in Uganda, v / Varese
U come Uganda, Vi / Varese
oo koh-meh oo-gahn-dah, vee / vah-reh-seh

w as in Washington
Vi doppia come Washington
vee dohp-pee-ah koh-meh washington

x as in Xenia
Ics come Xenia
eeks koh-meh kseh-nee-ah

y as in York, z / Zara
Ipsilon come York, Zeta / Zara
ee-psee-lohn koh-meh york, tseh-tah / tsah-rah

Where's the (Alitalia) office?
Dov'è l'ufficio dell'(Alitalia)?
*doh-**veh** loof-**fee**-choh dehl-(lah-lee-**tah**-lee-ah)*

When does ...?
A che ora ...?
*ah keh **oh**-rah ...*

... the next plane leave for ...
... parte il prossimo aereo per ...
*... **pahr**-teh eel **prohs**-see-moh ah-**eh**-re-hoh pehr*

When does it arrive?
A che ora arriva?
*ah keh **oh**-rah ahr-**ree**-vah*

How long is it delayed?
Di quanto è in ritardo?
*dee **kwhan**-toh **eh** een ree-**tahr**-doh*

I have lost my ticket!
Ho perso il biglietto!
***oh pehr**-soh **eel** beel-**yeht**-toh*

I have missed my plane!
Ho perso l'aereo!
***oh pehr**-soh lah-**eh**-reh-oh*

Is there another flight, please?
C'è un altro volo, per favore?
*cheh oon **ahl**-troh **voh**-loh, pehr fah-**voh**-reh*

I'd like to book a seat
Vorrei prenotare un posto
*vohr-**reh**-ee preh-noh-**tah**-reh oon **poh**-stoh*

I would like to alter my ...
Vorrei cambiare la mia ...
*vohr-**reh**-ee kahm-bee-**ah**-reh lah **mee**-ah ...*

... reservation to ...
... prenotazione per ...
*... preh-noh-tah-tsee-**oh**-neh **pehr** ...*

Show me the calendar
Mi mostri il calendario
*mee **moh**-stree **eel** kah-lehn-**dah**-ree-oh*

I would like an upgrade on ...
Vorrei un aggiornamento su ...
*vohr-**reh**-ee oon ahj-johr-nah-**mehn**-toh soo*

... this is my ticket
... questo è il mio biglietto
*... **kweh**-stoh **eh** eel **mee**-oh beel-**yeht**-toh*

My luggage has not arrived ...
Il mio bagaglio non è arrivato ...
*eel **mee**-oh bah-**gal**-yoh nohn **eh** ahr-ree-**vah**-toh*

Please deliver it ...
Per favore, lo faccia pervenire ...
*pehr fah-**voh**-reh, loh **fahch**-ah pehr-veh-**nee**-reh*

... to my hotel
... al mio albergo
*... ahl **mee**-oh ahl-**behr**-goh*

... immediately it arrives
... appena arriva
*... ahp-**peh**-nah ahr-**ree**-vah*

Is there a courtesy bus ...?
C'è un autobus (gratuito) ...?
***cheh** oon **ou**-toh-boos (grah-**too**-ee-toh) ...*

... to the hotel
... per l'albergo
*... pehr lahl-**behr**-goh*

Is there a bus to the town?
C'è un autobus per la città?
cheh** oon **ou**-toh-boos pehr lah cheet-**tah

43

I have nothing to declare
Non ho niente da dichiarare
*nohn **oh** nee-**ehn**-teh dah dee-kee-ah-**rah**-reh*

I would like to declare these items
Vorrei dichiarare queste cose
*vohr-**reh**-ee dee-kee-ah-**rah**-reh **kweh**-steh
koh-zeh*

I am on holiday
Sono (in ferie) / in vacanza
soh-noh (een **feh**-ree-eh) / een vah-**kahn**-tsah*

I am on business
Sono in viaggio di lavoro
soh-noh een vee-**ah**-joh dee lah-**voh**-roh*

I am here for a few days
Sono qui per pochi giorni
soh-noh **kwee** pehr **poh**-kee **johr**-nee*

We are visiting friends
Visitiamo amici
*vee-see-**teeah**-moh ah-**mee**-chee*

Is there a boat to ...?
C'è una barca per ...?
cheh **oo**-*nah* **bahr**-*kah* **pehr** ...

At which ports do we stop?
In quali porti si fa scalo?
een **kwah**-*lee* **pohr**-*tee see fah* **skah**-*loh*

I'd like ...
Vorrei ...
*voh-**reh**-ee* ...

... to take a cruise
... fare una crociera
... ***fah**-reh* **oo**-*nah kroh-**cheh**-rah*

... a single cabin
... una cabina singola
... **oo**-*nah kah-**bee**-nah* **seen**-*goh-lah*

... a double cabin
... una cabina doppia
... **oo**-*nah kah-**bee**-nah* **dohp**-*pee-ah*

How much does it cost?
Quanto costa?
***kwahn**-toh* **koh**-*stah*

How many berths are there in this cabin?
Quante cuccette ci sono in questa cabina?
kwhan-teh *koo*-cheht-**teh** *chee* **soh**-*noh een*
kweh-s*tah kah-**bee**-nah*

Are there special prices for ...? *(see page 24)*
Ci sono prezzi speciali per ...?
chee **soh**-*noh* **preht**-*tsee speh-**chah**-lee pehr*

May I have a timetable?
Potrei avere la tabella degli orari?
*poh-**treh**-ee ah-**veh**-reh* **lah** *tah-**behl**-lah*
dehl-*yee oh-**rah**-ree*

When does the next boat leave?
A che ora parte la prossima barca?
ah keh **oh**-*rah* **pahr**-*teh lah* **prohs**-*see-mah*
bahr-*kah*

How often do the boats leave?
Ogni quanto partono le barche?
ohn-*yee* **kwahn**-*toh* **pahr**-*toh-noh leh* **bahr**-*keh*

... the (car) ferry
... il traghetto (per le automobili)
... *eel trah-**geht**-toh (**pehr leh**
*ah-oo-toh-**moh**-bee-lee)*

46

... the hydrofoil
... l'idroscafo
... *lee-droh-**skah**-foh*

How long ...?
Quanto ...?
***kwahn**-toh ...*

... is this ticket valid
... dura questo biglietto
... ***doo**-rah **kweh**-stoh bee-**lyet**-toh*

... do we stay in port?
... tempo si rimane nel porto?
... ***tehm**-poh see ree-**mah**-neh nehl **pohr**-toh*

... does it take to ...?
... si impiega per ...?
... *see eem-pee-**eh**-gah pehr ...*

Are refreshments available on board?
Ci sono rinfreschi a bordo?
*chee **soh**-noh reen-**freh**-skee ah **bohr**-doh*

Where are the toilets?
Dove sono i gabinetti?
***doh**-veh **soh**-noh ee gah-bee-**neht**-tee*

Excuse me ...
Mi scusi ...
*mee **skoo**-zee ...*

... may I use your phone? (your mobile phone)
... potrei usare il telefono?
(il suo telefonino)
*... poh-**treh**-ee oo-**zah**-reh eel teh-**leh**-foh-noh*
*(eel **soo**-oh teh-leh-foh-**nee**-noh)*

... my car has broken down
... la mia macchina ha un guasto
*lah **mee**-ah **mahk**-kee-nah **ah** oon **gwah**-stoh*

Can you tell me ...?
Potrebbe dirmi ...?
*poh-**trehb**-beh **deer**-mee ...*

... where's the nearest garage
... dov'è l'officina più vicina
*... doh-**veh** lof-fee-**chee**-nah pee-**oo**
vee-**chee**-nah*

... the motorway rescue number
... il numero del servizio recupero autostradale
*eel **noo**-meh-roh dehl sehr-**veet**-see-oh
reh-**koo**-peh-roh ah-oo-toh-strah-**dah**-leh*

Please write it down
Per favore, me lo scriva
pehr fah-***voh***-reh, *meh loh* ***skree***-vah

I've had a breakdown at ...
Ho avuto un guasto a ...
oh ah-***voo***-toh oon ***gwah***-stoh ah ...

Can you send ..?
Potrebbe mandare ..?
poh-***trehb***-beh mahn-***dah***-reh ...

... a mechanic
... un meccanico
... oon mehk-***kan***-ee-koh

... a tow truck
... un carro attrezzi
... oon ***kahr***-roh aht-***tred***-zee

I've run out of petrol
Sono rimasto senza benzina
soh-noh ree-***mah***-stoh ***sehn***-tsah behnt-***see***-na

The engine is overheating
Il motore si surriscalda
eel moh-***toh***-reh see soor-ree-***skal***-dah

The fan belt has broken
La cintura della ventola si è rotta
*lah cheen-**too**-rah **dehl**-lah **vehn**-toh-lah*
*see **eh roht**-tah*

It will not start
Il motore non si innesta
*eel moh-**toh**-reh nohn see een-**neh**-stah*

The tyre is flat
Ho una gomma a terra
***oh oo**-nah **gohm**-mah ah **tehr**-rah*

How much will it cost?
Quanto verrà a costare?
***kwahn**-toh vehr-**rah** ah koh-**stah**-reh*

How long will you be?
Tra quanto arriverà?
*trah **kwahn**-toh ahr-ree-veh-**rah***

When will it be ready?
Quando sarà pronta (la macchina)?
***kwahn**-doh sah-**rah prohn**-tah (lah
mahk-kee-nah)*

I've got a puncture
Ho forato una gomma
*oh foh-**rah**-toh oo-nah **gohm**-ma*

The engine water is boiling
L'acqua del motore bolle
***lahk**-kwah dehl moh-**toh**-reh **bohl**-leh*

There is something wrong with ...
C'è qualcosa che non va con ...
***cheh** kwahl-**kos**ah keh nohn vah ...*

... the alternator (battery)
... il trasformatore (la batteria)
***eel** trahs-fohr-mah-**toh**-reh (lah baht-teh-**ree**-ah)*

... the back lights
... i fanali posteriori
*... **ee** fah-**nah**-lee poh-steh-ree-**oh**-ree*

... the brakes
... i freni
*... ee **freh**-nee*

... the carburettor
... il carburatore
*... **eel** kahr-boo-rah-**toh**-reh*

... the clutch
... la frizione
... *lah free-tsee-**oh**-neh*

... the cooling system
... il sistema di raffreddamento
*eel sees-**teh**-mah dee rahf-fred-dah-**mehn**-toh*

... the electric system
... il sistema elettrico
... ***eel** see-**steh**-mah eh-**leht**-tree-koh*

... the front lights
... i fanali anteriori
... ***ee** fah-**nah**-lee ahn-teh-ree-**oh**-ree*

... fuel injection
... l'iniezione
... *lee-nee-eh-tsee-oh-neh*

... the gear box
... il cambio
... ***eel kahm**-bee-oh*

... the handbrake
... il freno a mano
... *eel **freh**-noh ah **mah**-noh*

... the heating system
... il sistema di riscaldamento
*eel sees-**teh**-mah dee ree-skahl-dah-**mehn**-toh*

... the oil pressure
... la pressione dell'olio
... ***lah** prehs-see-**oh**-neh dehl-l**ohl**-yoh*

... the radiator
... il radiatore
... ***eel** rah-dee-ah-**toh**-reh*

... the starter motor
... il motorino di accensione
***eel** moh-toh-**ree**-noh dee a-chehn-see-**oh**-neh*

... the steering wheel
... lo sterzo
... *loh **stehr**-tsoh*

... the (brakes) transmission
... la trasmissione (dei freni)
***lah** trahz-**mees**-see-oh-neh (**deh**-ee **freh**-nee)*

... the windscreen wipers
... i tergicristallo
... ***ee** tehr-gee-kree-**stahl**-loh*

I had an accident
Ho avuto un incidente
oh ah-***voo***-toh oon een-chee-***dehn***-teh

My car is smashed
La mia macchina è sfasciata
*lah **mee**-ah **mahk**-kee-nah **eh** sfah-**sha**-tah*

Could you send ...?
Potreste mandare ...?
*poh-**treh**-steh mahn-**dah**-reh ...*

... a tow truck, please
... un carro attrezzi
*... oon **kahr**-roh aht-**treh**-dzee*

I drove off the road ...
Sono uscito fuori strada ...
***soh**-noh oo-**shee**-toh foo-**oh**-ree **strah**-dah*

... and I am stuck ...
... e mi sono incastrato ...
*... eh mee **soh**-noh een-cah-**strah**-toh ...*

... with my car
... con la macchina
*... **kohn** lah **mak**-kee-nah*

My front windscreen ... is smashed
Il mio parabrezza ... è rotto
*eel **mee**-oh pah-rah-**brehd**-zah ... **eh roht**-toh*

... my side / back windscreen
... il mio finestrino laterale / posteriore
*eel **mee**-oh fee-neh-**stree**-noh lah-teh-**rah**-leh / poh-steh-ree-**oh**-reh*

I've locked myself out from my car
Mi sono chiuso fuori dalla macchina
*mee **soh**-noh kee-**oo**-zoh **fwoh**-ree **dahl**-lah **mahk**-kee-nah*

I've left the key inside
Ho lasciato la chiave dentro
*oh lah-**shah**-toh lah kee-**ah**-veh **dehn**-troh*

Could you come and help me?
Potreste venire ad aiutarmi?
*poh-**treh**-steh veh-**nee**-reh ahd a-ee-oo-**tahr**-mee*

How much would it cost?
Quanto verrà a costare?
***kwahn**-toh vehr-**rah** ah koh-**stah**-reh*

55

Never, ever, park in front of dustbins or containers.
In the event that your car is clamped or towed away, contact the
POLIZIA MUNICIPALE or **VIGILI URBANI**. Then say: La mia macchina è stata bloccata / rimossa. Che cosa devo fare? Devo pagare una multa? Di quanto? and wait for instructions.

My car has been clamped / towed away. What am I to do? Do I have to pay a fine? For how much?

*Lah **mee**-ah **mahk**-kee-nah **eh stah**-tah blohk-**kah**-tah / ree-**mohs**-sah. Keh **koh**-sah **deh**-vo **fah**-reh? **Deh**-voh pah-**gah**-reh **oo**-nah **mool**-tahh? Dee **kwahn**-toh?*

ACCENDERE I FARI PRIMA DI ENTRARE NEL TUNNEL
Switch on headlights
before entering tunnel

AREA (STAZIONE) DI SERVIZIO
Service area

ATTENZIONE!
Careful!

ATTENTI AL CANE
Beware of the dog

CADUTA MASSI
Falling rocks

CHIUSO
Closed

DISCO ORARIO
Parking disc required

DIVERSIONE
Diversion

DIVIETO DI ACCESSO
No admittance

DIVIETO DI CAMPEGGIO
No camping

DIVIETO DI FERMATA
No stopping

**DIVIETO DI PARCHEGGIO/di SOSTA
(PENA IL BLOCCO DELLE RUOTE)**
No parking (clamping zone)

DIVIETO DI SCARICO
No dumping

DOGANA
Customs

LAVORI IN CORSO
Road works

MANTENERE LA DESTRA
Keep right

MANTENERE LA SINISTRA
Keep left

PARCHEGGIO A PAGAMENTO
Pay and Display

PARCHEGGIO DI EMERGENZA
Emergency parking

PERICOLO
Danger

PROPRIETÀ' PRIVATA
Private property

RALLENTARE
Reduce speed

SENSO UNICO
One-way

STOP
Stop

ZONA PEDONALE
Pedestrian area

ZONA DI RIMOZIONE FORZATA
Towaway zone

Car hire
Autonoleggio
*ah-oo-toh-noh-**leh**-joh*

I'd like to hire ...
Vorrei noleggiare ...
*vohr-**reh**-ee noh-leh-**jah**-reh ...*

... a (small) car
... una (piccola) vettura
*... **oo**-nah (**peek**-koh-lah) veht-**too**-rah*

... medium-sized, large
... di media grandezza, grande
*dee **meh**-dee-ah grahn-**det**-sah, **grahn**-deh*

... automatic
... col cambio automatico
*... kohl **kahm**-bee-oh ou-toh-**mah**-tee-koh*

I'd like to hire it here ...
Vorrei noleggiarla qui...
*vohr-**reh**-ee noh-leh-**jahr**-lah **kwee** ...*

... and leave it in Savona
... e lasciarla a Savona
*... eh lah-**shahr**-lah ah sah-**voh**-nah*

I'd like it for (a day)
La vorrei per (un giorno)
*lah vohr-**reh**-ee pehr (oon **johr**-noh)*

... a week
... una settimana
... ***oo**-nah seht-tee-**mah**-nah*

... two, three, four, five
... due, tre, quattro, cinque
... ***doo**-eh, treh, **kwaht**-troh, **cheen**-kweh*

... six days, a weekend
... sei giorni, un fine settimana
***seh**-ee **johr**-nee, oon **fee**-neh seht-tee-**mah**-nah*

What's the charge ...?
Quant'è la retta ...?
*kwahn-**teh** lah **reht**-tah ...*

... per day (week)
... giornaliera (settimanale)
*johr-nah-lee-**eh**-rah (seht-tee-mah-**nah**-leh)*

What's the deposit?
Quant'è la caparra / il deposito?
*kwahn-**teh** lah kah-**pahr**-rah / eel deh-**poh**-zee-toh*

Are there special offers?
Avete offerte speciali?
ah-veh-teh ohf-fehr-teh speh-cha-lee

... weekend arrangements
... per il fine settimana
... pehr eel fee-neh seht-tee-mah-nah

... kilometres (mileage) included?
... chilometri (miglia) inclusi?
... kee-loh-meht-ree (meel-yah) een-kloo-zee

I want ...
Vorrei ...
vohr-reh-ee ...

... a second set of keys
... delle chiavi di riserva
... dehl-leh kee-ah-vee dee ree-sehr-vah

... full insurance
... un'assicurazione completa
oon-ahs-see-koo-raht-see-oh-neh kohm-pleh-tah

... personal accident
... per incidentia carico proprio
pehr een-chee-dehn-tee-ah kah-ree-koh proh-pree-o

Here's (my passport)
Quest è (il mio passaporto)
*kweh-steh **eh** (eel meeoh pahs-sah-**pohr**-toh)*

... home address
... indirizzo (domiciliare)
... *een-dee-**reet**-soh (doh-mee-chee-lee-**ah**-reh)*

.. my driving licence
... la mia patente di guida
.. *lah meeah pah-**tehn**-teh dee **gwee**-dah*

Can I take it ... across the border?
Posso portarla ... oltre confine?
***pohs**-soh pohr-**tahr**-lah ohl-treh-kohn-**fee**-neh*

.. (across) the French border?
.. (oltre) il confine francese?
*(ohl-treh) eel kohn-**fee**-neh frahn-**cheh**-zeh*

.. the Swiss border?
.. il confine svizzero?
.. *eel kohn-**fee**-neh **zveet**-seh-roh*

.. the Austrian border?
.. il confine austriaco?
.. *eel kohn-**fee**-neh ou-**stree**-ah-koh*

For city buses you generally buy books of tickets (blocchetti di biglietti) from newsagents and tobacco shops. For coaches you buy tickets at the bus or coach station (Stazione delle Corriere) or from the driver.
The urban or local bus is known as the autobus while the long-distance coach is known as the corriera.

Excuse me, where can I ...?
Mi scusi, dove posso...?
*mee **skoo**-zee, **doh**-veh **pohs**-soh*

... buy bus tickets
... comprare dei biglietti per l'autobus
*...kohm-**prah**-reh **deh**-ee beel-**yeht**-tee pehr **lah**-oo-toh-boos*

Do I stamp them on the bus?
Si convalidano sull'autobus?
*see kohn-**vah**-lee-dah-noh sool-**lah**-oo-toh-boo*

... automatically?
... automaticamente?
*... ah-oo-toh-mah-tee-kah-**mehn**-teh*

Where is ...?
Dov'è ...?
*doh-**veh***

... the bus station
... la stazione degli autobus
*lah staht-see-**oh**-neh **dehl**-yee ah-oo-toh-boos*

... the coach station
... la stazione delle corriere
*lah staht-see-**oh**-neh **dehl**-leh kohr-ree-**eh**-reh*

... the ticket office
... la biglietteria
... *lah bee-lyee-et-teh-**ree**-ah*

... the ticket machine
... la biglietteria automatica
*lah beel-yeht-teh-**ree**-ah ah-oo-toh-**mah**-tee-kah*

... the bus (coach) stop for ...
... la fermata per ...
... *lah fehr-**mah**-tah pehr ...*

Where is the platform for ...?
Dov'è il binario per ...?
*doh-**veh** eel bee-**nah**-ree-oh pehr ...*

Do you have a ...?
Avrebbe una ...?
*ahv-**rehb**-beh **oo**-nah ...*

... map
... carta geografica
... ***kahr**-tah jeh-oh-**grah**-fee-kah*

... timetable, please
... lista degli orari, per cortesia
***lee**-stah **del**-yee oh-**rah**-ree, pehr cohr-teh-**zee**-a*

Please show me ...
Per favore, mi mostri ...
*pehr fah-**voh**-reh, mee **moh**-stree ...*

... where we are
... dove siamo
... ***doh**-veh see-**ah**-moh*

How far is it to ...?
Quanto dista ...?
***kwahn**-toh **dee**-stah ...*

How much is the fare?
Quanto costa il tragitto?
***kwahn**-toh **koh**-stah eel trah-**jeet**-toh*

Where does the bus go from?
Da dove parte l'autobus?
*dah **doh**-veh **pahr**-teh lah-oo-toh-boos*

*lah-oo-toh-boos pehr...see **fehr**-mah lah*
L'autobus per...si ferma là
The bus to ... stops over there

How much does a ... cost? *(see next page)*
Quanto costa un ...?
***kwahn**-toh **koh**-stah oon ...*

Is there a reduction for ...
C'è una riduzione per ...
***cheh** oo-nah ree-doot-see-**oh**-neh pehr ...*

... disabled, groups
... i disabili, i gruppi
*... ee deez-**ah**-bee-lee, ee **groop**-pee*

... pensioners
... i pensionati
*... ee pehn-see-oh-**nah**-tee*

... students, children
... gli studenti, i bambini
*... ly stoo-**dehn**-tee, ee bahm-**bee**-nee*

I'd like a (single) ...
Vorrei un biglietto singolo ...
*vor-**reh**-ee oon beel-**yeht**-toh **seen**-goh-loh*

... return ticket
... biglietto di andata e ritorno
*beel-**yeht**-toh dee ahn-**dah**-tah eh ree-**tohr**-noh*

... a (round trip), carnet
... un (biglietto circolare), carnet
*oon (beel-**yeht**-toh cheer-koh-**lah**-reh) kahr-**neh***

... booklet (or a carnet, see above)
... un blocchetto di biglietti
*... oon blohk-**keht**-toh dee beel-**yeht**-tee*

Could you tell me ... (at what time) ...?
Potrebbe dirmi ... (a che ora) ... ?
*poh-**trehb**-beh **deer**-mee ... (ah keh **oh**-rah) ...*

... is the next bus ...
... è il prossimo autobus ...
*... **eh** eel **prohs**-see-moh ah-oo-toh-boos ...*

... (next coach) to ...
... (la prossima corriera) per ...
*(lah **prohs**-see-mah kohr-ree-**eh**-rah) pehr ...*

... is (the last bus) from ...?
... è (l'ultimo autobus) da ...?
... *eh (**lool**-tee-moh ah-oo-toh-boos) dah*

... (the last coach) from ...
... (l'ultima corriera) da ...
... *(**lool**-tee-mah kohr-ree**eh**-rah) dah ...*

... when to get off
... quando devo scendere
... ***kwahn**-doh **deh**-voh **shehn**-deh-reh*

Does this coach stop at ...?
Si ferma a ... questa corriera?
*see **fehr**-mah ah ... **kweh**-stah kohr-ree-**eh**-rah*

... the airport
... all'aereoporto
... *ahl-lah-**eh**-reh-oh-**pohr**-toh*

How long does it take ...?
Quanto si impiega ...?
***kwahn**-toh see eem-pee-**eh**-gah ...*

... to get there (from here)
... ad arrivare (da di qua)
... *ahd ahr-ree-vah-reh (dah dee kwah)*

How long is this ticket valid?
Quanto dura il biglietto?
kwahn-toh doo-rah eel beel-yeht-toh

We want to make a city sightseeing tour
Vogliamo fare un giro
turistico della città.
vohl-yah-moh fah-reh oon jee-roh
too-ree-stee-koh dehl-lah cheet-tah

Are there organised tours?
Ci sono gite organizzate?
chee soh-noh jee-teh ohr-gah-need-zah-teh

Does the bus call at the ... hotel
L'autobus si ferma all'hotel (albergo) ...?
lah-oo-toh-boos (lah kohr-ree-eh-rah) see
fehr-mah ahll-oh-tehle (ahl-behr-goh) ...

deh-veh prehn-deh-reh oon noo-meh-roh ...
Deve prendere un numero ...
You must take a number ...

The buses run every ten minutes
Gli autobus vanno ogni dieci minuti
lyee ah-oo-toh-boos vahn-noh ohn-yee
dee-eh-chee mee-noo-tee

Can I pay the driver?
Posso pagare all'autista?
*pos-soh pah-**gah**-reh ahll-ah-oo-**tee**-stah*

I have some luggage ...
Avrei del bagaglio ...
*ahv-**reh**-ee dehl bah-**gah**-lyoh ...*

... to put in the boot
... da mettere nel bagagliaio
*dah **meht**-teh-reh nehl bah-gahl-yee-**ah**-ee-oh*

Excuse me ...
Mi scusi ...
*mee **skoo**-zee ...*

... would you tell me ...
... potrebbe avvertirmi ...
*... poh-**trehb**-beh ahv-vehr-**teer**-mee ...*

... when we arrive ...
... quando arriviamo ...
*... **kwahn**-doh ahr-ree-vee-**ah**-moh ...*

... at the ... stop
... alla fermata di ...
*... **ahl**-lah fehr-**mah**-tah dee ...*

Sorry, I feel sick ...
Mi scusi, mi sento male ...
*mee **skoo**-zee, mee **sehn**-toh **mah**leh*

My friend is feeling sick ...
Il mio amico si sente male ...
*eel **mee**-oh ah-**mee**-koh see **sehn**-teh **mah**-leh*

... could you stop please?
... potrebbe fermarsi?
*... poh-**trehb**-beh fehr-**mahr**-see*

... as soon as possible
... al più presto
*... ahl pee-**oo preh**-stoh*

IMMEDIATELY, IT'S AN EMERGENCY!
Subito! È un'emergenza!
***soo**-bee-toh! **eh** oon-eh-mehr-**gehn**-tsah*

Would you give me ...?
Potrebbe darmi ...?
*poh-**trehb**-beh **dahr**-mee ...*

... my luggage, please
... il bagaglio, per favore
*... eel bah-**gah**-lyoh, pehr fah-**voh**-reh*

Where can I get a taxi ...?
Dove posso prendere un taxi?
doh-veh pohs-soh prehn-deh-reh oon tahk-see

Please get me a taxi
Per favore, mi chiami un taxi
pehr fah-voh-reh, mee kee-ah-mee oon tahk-see

Are you free?
È libero?
eh lee-beh-roh

I'm in a hurry
Sono di fretta
soh-noh dee freht-tah

What's the fare to ...?
Quant'è la tariffa per ...?
kwahn-teh lah tah-reef-fah pehr ...

How far is it to ...?
Quanto lontano è ...?
kwahn-toh lohn-tah-noh eh ...

Take me to ...
Mi porti a ...
mee pohr-tee ah ...

... to this address
... a questo indirizzo
... *ah **kweh**-stoh een-dee-**reet**-tsoh*

... the centre of the town
... al centro
... *ahl **chehn**troh*

... the railway station
... alla stazione ferroviaria
***ahl**-lah sta-tsee-**oh**-neh fehr-roh-vee-**ah**-ree-ah*

... bus to ..., train to ...
... l'autobus per ..., il treno per ...
*lah-oo-toh-boos pehr ..., eel **treh**-noh pehr ...*

... the ... airport
... all'aereoporto ...
... *ahl-lah-**eh**-reh-oh-**pohr**-toh ...*

... international ...
... internazionale
... *een-tehr-nah-tsee-oh-**nah**-leh*

Would you let me alight here?
Potrebbe farmi scendere qui?
*poh-**trehb**-beh **fahr**-mee **shehn**-deh-reh kwee*

Could you wait for me?
Potrebbe aspettarmi?
*poh-**trehb**-beh ah-speht-**tahr**-mee*

I'll be back in 15 minutes
Tornerò tra quindici minuti
*tohr-neh-**roh** trah **kween**-dee-chee mee-**noo**-tee*

5, 10, 20 minutes
cinque, dieci, venti minuti
***cheen**-kweh, dee-**eh**-chee, **vehn**-tee mee-**noo**-tee*

a quarter of an hour / half an hour
un quarto d'ora / mezz'ora
*oon **kwahr**-toh **doh**-rah / mehdz-**oh**-rah*

three-quarters of an hour
tre quarti d'ora
*treh **kwahr**-tee **doh**-rah*

Could you help me ...?
Potrebbe aiutarmi ...?
*Poh-**trehb**-beh ah-ee-oo-**tahr**-mee*

.. to carry my luggage
... a portare il bagaglio
*.. ah pohr-**tah**-reh eel bah-**gah**-lee-yoh*

Where's the nearest ...?
Dov'è la più vicina ...?
doh-veh la pee-oo vee-chee-nah ...

... Metro station
... stazione della metropolitana
stat-see-oh-neh dehl-lah meht-roh-poh-lee-tah-nah

Excuse me, where is the ticket office?
Mi scusi, dov'è la biglietteria?
mee skoo-zee, doh-veh lah beel-yeht-teh-ree-ah

Where can I ...?
Dove potrei ...?
doh-veh poh-treh-ee ...

... get change for ...
... ottenere delle monete per ...
oht-teh-neh-reh dehl-leh moh-neh-teh pehr

... the ticket machine
... la biglietteria automatica
lah beel-yeht-teh-ree-ah ah-oo-toh-mah-tee-ka

I'd like ...
Vorrei ...
vohr-reh-ee ...

... a (one way) ticket
... un biglietto (di sola andata)
*oon bee-ly-**eht**-toh (dee **soh**-lah ahn-**dah**-tah)*

... a return (to) ...
... di andata e ritorno (per) ...
*... dee ahn-**dah**-tah eh ree-**tohr**-noh (pehr) ...*

Is there a reduction for ... *(see page 24)*
C'è una riduzione per ...
*cheh **oo**nah ree-doot-see-**oh**-neh pehr ...*

How long is this ticket valid?
Quanto dura il biglietto?
***kwahn**-toh **doo**-rah eel beel-**yeht**-toh*

Which line should I take for ...?
Che linea dovrei prendere per ...?
*keh **lee**-neh-ah dohv-**reh**-ee **prehn**-deh-reh pehr*

Where is the platform for ...?
Dov'è il binario per ...?
*doh-**veh** eel bee-**nah**-ree-oh pehr ...*

Does this train go to ...?
Questo treno va a ...?
***kweh**-stoh **treh**-noh vah ah ...*

Is the next station ...?
La prossima stazione è ...?
*lah **prohs**-see-mah stah-tsee-**oh**-neh **eh** ...*

Where is there a map?
C'è una mappa da consultare?
***cheh** oo-nah **mahp**-pah dah kohn-sool-**tah**-reh*

... please show me ...
... per favore, mi mostri ...
*... pehr fah-**voh**-reh, mee **moh**-stree ...*

... where we are
... dove siamo
*... **doh**-veh see-**ah**-moh*

Where do I change for ...?
Dove si cambia per ...?
***doh**-veh see **kahm**-bee-ah pehr ...*

Does this train stop at ...?
Si ferma a ... questo treno?
*see **fehr**-mah ah ... **kweh**-stoh **treh**-noh*

... the train stop for ...?
... la fermata per ...?
*... lah fehr-**mah**-tah pehr ...*

How long does it take ...?
Quanto si impiega ...?
kwahn-toh see eem-pee-eh-gah ...

... to get there (from here)
... ad andare là (da di qua)
... ahd ahn-dah-reh lah (dah dee kwah)

At what time is ...?
A che ora è ...?
ah keh oh-rah eh ...

... the next train to ...
... il prossimo treno per ...
... eel prohs-see-moh treh-noh pehr ...

... the last train for ...
... l'ultimo treno per ...
... lool-tee-moh treh-noh pehr ...

... the last train from ...?
... l'ultimo treno da ...?
... lool-tee-moh treh-noh dah ...

chee soh-noh treh-nee ohn-yee treh mee-noo-tee
Ci sono treni ogni tre minuti
There are trains every three minutes

*kwahn-toh tehm-poh vee fehr-**mah**-teh*
Quanto tempo vi fermate?
How long are you staying here?

I'll be staying ...
Mi fermerò per ...
*mee fehr-meh-**roh** pehr ...*

... a few days
... qualche giorno
*... **kwahl**-keh **johr**-noh*

... a week, a month
... una settimana, un mese
*... **oo**-nah seht-tee-**mah**-nah, oon **meh**-zeh*

I don't know yet
Non so ancora
*nohn soh ahn-**koh**-rah*

*kwahl-**eh** eel **soo**-oh een-dee-**reet**-tsoh ...*
Qual'è il suo indirizzo ...?
What is your address ...?

*... een ee-**tah**-lee-ah*
... in Italia
... in Italy

My address here is ...
Il mio indirizzo qui è ...
*eel **mee**-oh een-dee-**reet**-tsoh **kwee** eh ...*

I'm here (on business) ...
Sono qui (per lavoro) ...
***soh**-noh kwee (pehr lah-**voh**-roh)*

*see-**eh**-teh een-see-**eh**-meh*
Siete insieme?
Are you together?

I'm travelling (alone) on holiday
Viaggio (solo) in vacanza
*vee-**ahj**-joh (**soh**-loh) een vah-**kahn**-tsah*

... with my wife
... con mia moglie
*...kohn **mee**-ah **mohl**-yeh*

... with my family
... con la mia famiglia
*...kohn lah **mee**-ah fah-**meel**-yah*

... a friend (male / female)
... un amico / un'amica
*... oon ah-**mee**-koh / oon-ah-**mee**-kah*

I have (something to) ...
Ho (qualcosa da) ...
*oh (kwahl-**koh**-sah dah) ...*

... nothing to declare
... niente da dichiarare
*... nee-**ehn**-teh dah dee-kee-ah-**rah**-reh*

*Seen-**yoh**-rah/Seen-**yoh**-reh, ...*
Signora/Signore, ...
Madam / Sir, ...

*... **kwahn**-toh deh-**nah**-roh ah*
... quanto denaro ha?
... how much money have you?

... currency
... della valuta
*... **dehl**-lah vah-**loo**-tah*

... some pounds, some dollars
... delle sterline, dei dollari
*dehl-leh stehr-**lee**-neh, **deh**ee **dohl**-lah-ree*

This is my luggage
Questo è il mio bagaglio
*kweh-stoh eh eel **mee**-oh bah-**gahl**-yee-oh*

ah preh-pah-rah-toh leh-ee stehs-sah ...?
Ha preparato lei stessa ...?
Did you pack ... yourself?

ah teh-noo-toh lah vah-lee-jah ...
Ha tenuto (la valigia) ...?
Did you keep (the suitcase) ...?

... sehm-preh kohn seh
... sempre con sè
... with you all the time

It has only ...
Contiene solo ...
kohn-tee-eh-neh soh-loh ...

... my personal things in it
... i miei effetti personali
... ee mee-eh-ee ehf-feht-tee pehr-soh-nah-lee

vohr-rehb-beh seh-gweer-mee, pehr fah-voh-reh
Vorrebbe seguirmi, per favore?
Would you follow me, please?

vah beh-neh, vah-dah poo-reh
Va bene, vada pure
Very good, you can go

Is there ... near here?
C'è ... qui vicino?
*cheh ... kwee vee-**chee**-noh*

... a bar, a campsite ...
... un bar, un campeggio ...
*... oon bahr, oon kahm-**pehj**-joh ...*

... a bank, a pharmacy ...
... una banca, una farmacia ...
*... oo-nah **bahn**-kah, oo-nah fahr-mah-**chee**-ah*

... a hotel, a petrol station ...
... un albergo, un benzinaio ...
*... oon ahl-**behr**-goh, oon behn-tsee-**nah**-ee-oh*

... a post office ...
... un ufficio postale ...
*... oon oof-**fee**-choh poh-**stah**-leh ...*

... a restaurant ...
... un ristorante ...
*... oon ree-stoh-**rahn**-teh ...*

... a tourist office ...
... un ufficio turistico ...
*... oon oof-**fee**-choh too-**ree**-stee-koh ...*

Is it far to ...?
È lontano da ...?
eh lohn-tah-noh dah ...

... Doctor X' surgery
... l'ambulatorio del Dottor X
lahm-boo-lah-toh-ree-oh dehl doht-tohr X

... the dentist's surgery
... l'ambulatorio del dentista
lahm-boo-lah-toh-ree-oh dehl dehn-tee-stah

How many kilometres to ...?
Quanti chilometri fino a ...?
kwahn-tee kee-loh-meht-ree fee-noh ah ...

... the youth hostel
... l'ostello della gioventù
... loh-stehl-loh dehl-lah joh-vehn-too

Please show me ...
Per favore, mi mostri ...
pehr fah-voh-reh, mee moh-stree ...

... on this map ...
... su questa mappa ...
... soo kweh-stah mahp-pah ...

... where I am
... dove sono
... *doh-veh soh-noh*

... the art gallery
... la galleria d'arte
... *lah gahl-leh-ree-ah dahr-teh*

... the castle
... il castello
... *eel kah-stehl-loh*

... the cinema
... il cinema
... *eel chee-neh-mah*

... the museum
... il museo
... *eel moo-zeh-oh*

... the palace
... il palazzo
... *eel pah-laht-tsoh*

... the theatre
... il teatro
... *eel teh-ah-troh*

We want the motorway for ...
Vorremmo l'autostrada per ...
*vohr-**rehm**-moh lah-oo-toh-strah-dah **pehr***

Keep straight on ...
Continui diritto ...
*kohn-**tee**-noo-ee dee-**ree**-toh ...*

for ... (metres), kilometres
per ... (metri), chilometri
*pehr ... (**meht**-ree), kee-**loh**-meht-ree*

Turn right (left) ...
Gira a destra (a sinistra) ...
***Jee**-rah ah **deh**-strah (ah see-**nee**-strah) ...*

... at the (traffic lights), roundabout
... al semaforo, al rondello
*... ahl seh-**mah**-foh-roh, ahl rohn-**dehl**-loh*

... at the crossroads
... all'incrocio
*... ahll-een-**kroh**-choh*

... the end of the road
... alla fine della strada
*... **ahl**-lah **fee**-neh **dehl**-lah **strah**-dah*

May I have a map, ...?
Potrei avere una mappa, ...?
*poh-**treh**-ee ah-**veh**-reh **oo**-nah **mahp**-pah*

I'd like a street plan, ...
Vorrei una guida stradale, ...
*vohr-**reh**-ee **oo**-nah **gwee**-dah stra-**dah**-leh*

... please
... per cortesia
... *pehr kohr-teh-**zee**-ah*

How far is it to ...?
Quanto dista ...?
***kwahn**-toh **dee**-stah ...*

Where is (where are) ...?
Dov'è (dove sono) ...?
*do-**veh** (**doh**-veh **soh**-noh) ...*

... the nearest ...
... la più vicina ...
... *lah pee-**oo** vee-**chee**-nah ...*

... the airport
... l'aereoporto
... *lah-eh-reh-oh-**pohr**-toh*

... **the beach, a car park**
... la spiaggia, il parcheggio
... *lah spee-**ahj**-jah, eel pahr-**kehj**-joh*

... **the city centre**
... il centro cittadino
... *eel **chehn**-troh cheet-tah-**dee**-noh*

... **garage**
... officina
... *ohf-fee-**chee**-nah*

... **the golf course**
... il campo da golf
... *eel **kahm**-poh dah golf*

... **petrol station**
... stazione di servizio
... *stat-see-**oh**-neh dee sehr-**veet**-see-oh*

... **the railway station**
... la stazione ferroviaria
*lah stat-see-**oh**-neh fehr-roh-vee-**ah**-ree-ah*

... **the skating rink**
... la pista da pattinaggio
... *lah **pee**-stah dah paht-tee-**nahj**-joh*

... **the swimming pool, ski slope**
... la piscina, la pista da sci
... *lah pee-**shee**-nah, lah **pees**-tah **dah shee***

... **the tennis courts**
... i campi da tennis
... *ee **kahm**-pee dah tennis*

... **this address**
... questo indirizzo
... ***kweh**-stoh een-dee-**reet**-soh*

... **the tourist office**
... l'ufficio turistico
... *loof-**fee**-choh too-**ree**-steekoh*

Please, ...?
Per piacere, ...?
*pehr pee-ah-**cheh**-reh, ...*

... **will you show me**
... potrebbe mostrarmi
... *poh-**trehb**-beh moh-**strahr**-mee*

... **will you write it down for me**
... me lo scriva
... *meh loh **skree**-vah*

Liquid measure

1 litre = 1.761 Imperial pints
1 Imperial pint = 0.572 litre
1 Imperial gal = 4.551 litres

lit	5	10	15	20	25	30	35	40	45	50
gal	1.1	2.2	3.3	4.4	5.5	6.6	7.7	8.8	9.9	11

Distance

1 kilometre = 0.621 mile
1 mile = 1.609 km

km	10	20	30	40	50	60	70	80	90	100
mile	6	12	19	25	31	37	44	50	56	62

mile	10	20	30	40	50	60	70	80	90	100
km	16	32	48	64	80	97	113	129	145	161

Tyre pressures

psi	18	22	26	30	34	38	42	46	50
bar	1.27	1.55	1.83	2.11	2.39	2.67	2.95	3.24	3.52

psi	20	24	28	32	36	40	44	48	52
bar	1.41	1.69	1.97	2.25	2.53	2.81	3.09	3.38	3.66

Self-service
Self-service
*sehlf **sehr**-vees*

Super (premium), regular, unleaded, diesel
Super, normale, verde, diesel
***soo**-pehr, nohr-**mah**-leh, **vehr**-deh, **dee**-zehl*

Fill it up, please
Il pieno, per favore.
*eel pee-**eh**-noh, pehr fah-**voh**-reh*

... litres of petrol / diesel / gas
... litri di benzina / diesel / gas
*... **leet**-ree dee behn-**tsee**-nah / **dee**-zehl / gahz*

... lire' worth of petrol / diesel / gas
... lire di benzina / diesel / gas
*... **lee**-reh dee behn-**tsee**-nah / **dee**-zehl / gahz*

Would you ...?
Mi ... per favore?
*mee ... pehr fah-**voh**-reh*

... clean the windscreen
... pulirebbe il parabrezza ...
*... poo-lee-**rehb**-beh eel pah-rah-**brehd**-zah*

92

Please check (the oil)
Per favore, controlli (l'olio)
*pehr fah-**voh**-reh, kohn-**trohl**-lee (**lohl**-yoh)*

antifreeze / coolant, the battery
l'antigelo, la batteria
*lahn-tee-jeh-**loh**, lah baht-teh-**ree**-ah*

the brakes, the brake fluid
i freni, il liquido dei freni
*ee **freh**-nee, eel **lee**-kwee-doh **deh**ee **freh**-nee*

the fan belt
la cintura della ventola
*lah cheen-**too**-rah **dehl**-lah **vehn**-toh-lah*

the lightbulb, the spark plugs
la lampadina, le candele
*lah lahm-pah-**dee**-nah, leh kahn-**deh**-leh*

the pressure ...
la pressione ...
*lah prehs-see-**oh**-neh ...*

... of the tyre
... dei pneumatici
*... **deh**-ee pneh-oo-**mah**-tee-chee*

... and the spare tyre too
... e anche la ruota di scorta
*... eh **ahn**-keh lah **rwoh**-tah dee **skohr**-tah*

the water
l'acqua
***lahk**-kwah*

the windscreen washers
lo spruzzo per il parabrezza
*loh **sproot**-soh pehr eel pah-rah-**bredz**-tsah*

the windscreen wipers
i tergicristallo
*ee tehr-jee-kree-**stahl**-loh*

Please change the oil
Per favore cambi l'olio
*pehr fah-**voh**-reh, **kahm**-bee **lohl**-yoh*

Where are the toilets?
Dove sono i gabinetti?
***doh**-veh **soh**-noh ee gah-bee-**neht**-tee*

How much is it?
Quanto costa?
***kwahn**-toh **koh**-stah*

Where is ...? / Where are ...?
Dov'è ...? / Dove sono ...?
*doh-**veh** ... / doh-veh soh-noh ...*

... the lost property office
... l'ufficio oggetti smarriti
... *loof-**fee**-choh ohj-**jeht**-tee zmahr-**ree**-tee*

... the platform for ...
... il binario per ...
... *eel bee-**nah**-ree-oh pehr ...*

... the railway station
... la stazione ferroviaria
*lah stah-tsee-**oh**-neh fehr-roh-vee-**ah**-ree-ah*

... the snack bar, the telephones
... il bar, i telefoni
... *eel bahr, ee teh-**leh**-foh-nee*

... the ticket office
... la biglietteria
... *lah beel-yeht-teh-**ree**-ah*

... the toilets
... i gabinetti
... *ee gah-bee-**neht**-tee*

Nowadays, tickets must be validated by
inserting them into machines
(macchinette per la convalida /
*mahk-kee-**neht**-teh**pehr** lah kohn-**vah**-lee-dah*)
before you board the train

Excuse me, where is the (ticket office)?
Mi scusi, dov'è la (biglietteria)?
*mee **skoo**-zee, doh-**veh** lah (beel-yeht-teh-**ree**-ah)*

... validation machine
... macchinetta per la convalida
*mahk-kee-**neht**-tah **pehr** lah kohn-**vah**-lee-dah*

What's the fare to ...?
Quant'è la retta per ...?
*kwahn-**teh** lah **reht**-tah pehr ...*

Is there a reduction for ...? *(see page 24)*
C'è una riduzione per...?
***cheh oo**-nah ree-doo-tsee-**oh**-neh pehr ...*

Must I change trains?
Devo cambiare treno?
***deh**-voh kahm-bee-**ah**-reh **treh**-noh*

Is there a ... reservation?
C'è una ... prenotazione?
cheh oo-nah ... preh-noh-tah-tsee-oh-neh

... compulsory ...
... obbligatoria ...
... ohb-blee-gah-toh-ree-ah ...

... first-class supplement
... supplemento di prima classe
soop-pleh-mehn-toh dee pree-mah klahs-seh

... Intercity / express
... Intercity / espresso
... een-tehr-see-tee / ehs-prehs-soh

... regional / high speed
... regionale / ad alta velocità
reh-joh-nah-leh / ahd ahl-tah veh-loh-chee-tah

How long does it take ...?
Quanto si impiega ...?
kwahn-toh see eem-pee-eh-gah ...

... to get there from here
... ad andare là da di qua
... ahd ahn-dah-reh lah dah di kwah

I'd like ... (a ticket) to ...
Vorrei ... (un biglietto) per ...
*vohr-**reh**-ee ... (oon beel-**yeht**-toh) pehr*

... one-way to ...
... di sola andata per ...
*... dee **soh**-lah ahn-**dah**-tah pehr*

... single, round-trip
... singolo, circolare
*... **seen**-goh-loh, cheer-koh-**lah**-reh*

...' return to ...
... di andata e ritorno per ...
*... dee ahn-**dah**-tah eh ree-**tohr**-noh pehr*

... first (second) class
... di prima (seconda) classe
*... dee **pree**-mah (seh-**kohn**-dah) **klahs**-seh*

... with sleeper / couchette
... con cuccetta
*... kohn kooch-**cheht**-tah*

Must I validate the ticket?
Devo convalidare il biglietto?
***deh**-voh kohn-vah-lee-**dah**-reh eel beel-**yeht**-toh*

At what time does the ...
A che ora ...
*ah keh **oh**-rah ...*

... (next) train ...
... (il prossimo) treno ...
*... (eel **prohs**-see-moh) **treh**-noh ...*

... arrive (at) ...
... arriva (a) ...
*... ahr-**ree**-vah (ah) ...*

Is there a restaurant car?
C'è un vagone ristorante?
*cheh oon vah-**goh**-neh ree-stoh-**rahn**-teh*

Where is the platform for ...?
Dov'è il binario per ...?
*doh-**veh** eel bee-**nah**-ree-oh pehr ...*

Does this train stop at ...?
Si ferma a ... questo treno?
*see **fehr**-mah ah ... **kweh**-stoh **treh**-noh*

Is this seat taken?
È occupato questo sedile?
*eh ohk-koo-**pah**-toh kweh-stoh seh-**dee**-leh*

Is this (the right train for) ...?
È questo (il treno giusto per) ...?
*eh **kweh**-stoh (eel **treh**-noh **joo**-stoh pehr) ...*

... the train stop for ...?
... la fermata per ...?
*... lah fehr-**mah**-tah pehr ...*

At what time is ...?
A che ora è ...?
*ah keh **oh**-rah **eh** ...*

... the last train from (to) ...
... l'ultimo treno da (per) ...
*... **lool**-tee-moh **treh**-noh dah (pehr) ...*

... the next train (to) ...
... il prossimo treno (per) ...
*... eel **prohs**-see-moh **treh**-noh (pehr) ...*

There are trains every half hour
Ci sono treni ogni mezz'ora
*chee **soh**-noh **treh**-nee **ohn**-yee mehdz-**oh**-rah*

How long is this ticket valid?
Quanto dura il biglietto?
***kwahn**-toh **doo**-rah eel beel-**yeht**-toh*

Where's the tourist office?
Dov'è l'ufficio turistico?
*doh-**veh** loof-**fee**-choh too-**ree**-stee-koh*

What should one see here?
Che cosa c'è da visitare qui?
*keh **koh**-zah **cheh** dah vee-zee-**tah**-reh **kwee***

We're here for ... (half a day)
Siamo qui per ... mezza giornata
*see-**ah**-moh **kwee** pehr ... **mehd**-zah johr-**nah**-tah*

... the whole day
... tutto il giorno
*... **too**-toh eel **johr**-noh*

... the whole week
... tutta la settimana
*... **too**-tah lah seht-tee-**mah**-nah*

May I have ...?
Potrei avere ...?
*poh-**treh**-ee ah-**veh**-reh ...*

... a street plan
... una mappa stradale
*... **oo**-na **mahp**-pah strah-**dah**-leh*

101

We are most interested ...
Sopratutto siamo interessati ...
*soh-prah-**toot**-toh see-**ah**-moh een-teh-rehs-**sah**-tee*

... in antiques
... a antiquariato
*... ah ahn-tee-kwah-ree-**ah**-toh*

... in archaeology
... a archeologia
*... ah ahr-keh-oh-loh-**jee**-ah*

... in architecture, art
... a architettura, arte
*... ah ahr-kee-teht-**too**-rah, **ahr**-teh*

... in botany and gardens
... a botanica e giardini
*... ah boh-**tah**-nee-kah eh jahr-**dee**-nee*

... in cathedrals, churches
... a cattedrali, chiese
*... ah kaht-teh-**drah**-lee, kee-**eh**-zeh*

I'd like to see (visit) ...
Mi piacerebbe visitare ...
*mee pee-ah-cheh-**rehb**-beh vee-zee-**tah**-reh*

... **an art gallery**
... una galleria d'arte
... *oo-nah gahl-leh-**ree**-ah **dahr**-teh*

... **a library**
... una biblioteca
... *oo-nah bee-blee-oh-**teh**-kah*

... **a mausoleum, some monuments**
... un mausoleo, dei monumenti
*oon mah-oo-zoh-**leh**-oh, dehee moh-noo-**mehn**-tee*

... **natural history museums**
... musei di storia naturale
*moo-**zeh**-ee dee **stoh**-ree-ah nah-too-**rah**-leh*

... **the palace, the ruins, the zoo**
... il palazzo, le rovine, lo zoo
*eel pah-**laht**-soh, leh roh-**vee**-neh, loh zdoh*

What can you suggest ...?
Che cosa potrebbe suggerire ...?
*keh **koh**-zah poh-**trehb**-beh sooj-jeh-**ree**-reh*

... **for the children ...**
... per i bambini ...
... *pehr ee bahm-**bee**-nee ...*

... not too far away
... on troppo lontano
... *nohn **trohp**-poh lohn-**tah**-noh*

Have you a guide book (in English)?
Avrebbe una guida (in inglese)?
*ahv-**rehb**-beh **oo**-na **gwee**-dah (een een-**gleh**-zeh)*

I'd like a catalogue
Vorrei un catalogo
*vohr-**reh**-ee oon kah-**tah**-loh-goh*

Please show me
Per favore, mi mostri
*pehr fah-**voh**-reh, mee **moh**-stree*

At what time does it open (close)?
A che ora apre (chiude)?
*ah keh **oh**-rah **ah**-preh (kee-**oo**-deh)*

When are the ...?
A che ora è ...?
*ah keh **oh**-rah **eh** ...*

... last admissions
... l'ultima ammissione
... ***lool**-tee-mah ahm-mees-see-**oh**-neh*

How much is the entrance fee?
Quant'è il biglietto di entrata?
*kwahn-**teh** eel beel-**yeht**-toh dee ehn-**trah**-tah*

Is there a special price for ... *(see page 24)*
C'è un prezzo speciale per ...
*cheh oon **preht**-tsoh spe-**chah**-leh **pehr** ...*

Is there ... (a guide)?
C'è (una guida) ...?
*cheh (**oo**-nah **gwee**-dah) ...*

... English-speaking
... che parla inglese
*... keh **pahr**-lah een-**gleh**-zeh*

... recorded guides
... guide su nastro
*... goo-ee-deh soo **nah**-stroh*

Can I take pictures?
Posso fare fotografie?
***pohs**-soh **fah**-reh foh-toh-grah-**fee**-eh*

Can I use flash?
Posso usare il flash?
***pohs**-soh oo-**zah**-reh eel flahsh*

When was it built?
Quando è stato costruito?
kwahn-doh eh stah-toh coh-stroo-ee-toh

Who built it?
Chi lo ha costruito?
kee loh ah koh-stroo-ee-toh

Where's the house where ... lived?
Dov'è la casa dove ... è vissuto?
doh-veh lah kah-zah doh-veh ... leh vees-soo-toh

Where is ... male (female) buried?
Dov'è seppellito (seppellita) ...?
doh-veh sehp-pehl-lee-toh (sehp-pehl-lee-tah)

Who was ... (the architect)?
Chi era ... (l'architetto)?
kee eh-rah ... (lahr-kee-teht-toh)

... the painter, sculptor
... il pittore, lo scultore
... eel peet-toh-reh, loh skool-toh-reh

At what time is the service?
A che ora è il servizio?
ah keh oh-rah eh eel sehr-veet-see-oh

Where's the nearest ...?
Dov'è la più vicina ...?
*doh-**veh** lah pee-**oo** vee-**chee**-nah ...*

... travel agent
... agenzia turistica
... *ah-jehn-**tsee**-ah too-**ree**-stee-kah*

Is there a flight to ... on ...?
C'è un volo per ... ?
***cheh** oon **voh**-loh pehr ...*

Is it direct?
È diretto?
***eh** dee-**reht**-toh*

Must I change planes? Where?
Devo cambiare aereo? Dove?
***deh**-voh kam-bee-**ah**-reh ah-**eh**-reh-oh? **doh**-veh*

How far is it to ...?
Quanto dista ...?
***kwahn**-toh **dee**-stah ...*

... to the airport
... per l'aereoporto
*... pehr lah-eh-reh-oh-**pohr**-toh*

107

Is there a bus ...?
C'è un autobus ...?
cheh oon *ah-oo-toh-boos* ...

At what time does it ...
A che ora ...
ah keh **oh**-*rah* ...

... leave, arrive
... parte, arriva
... **pahr**-*tee, ahr-***ree**-*vah*

I'd like (to change) ...
Vorrei (cambiare) ...
*vohr-***reh**-*ee (kahm-bee-***ah**-*reh)* ...

... to cancel, to confirm ...
... annullare, confermare ...
... *ahn-nool-***lah**-*reh, kohn-fehr-***mah**-*reh* ...

... my reservation
... la mia prenotazione
... *lah* **mee**-*ah preh-noh-tat-see-***oh**-*neh*

What's the next flight to ...?
Quand'è il prossimo volo per ...?
*kwahn-***deh** *eel* **prohs**-*see-moh* **voh**-*loh pehr*

What's the (flight number) ...?
Qual'è (il numero di volo)...?
*kwah-**leh** (eel **noo**-meh-roh dee **voh**-loh) ...*

... check-in time
... l'ora del check-in
... *loh-rah dehl **chehk**-een*

I want (a single) to ...
Vorrei (una gita singola) per ...
*vohr-**reh**-ee (**oo**-nah **jee**-tah **seen**-goh-lah) pehr*

... return ticket ...
... biglietto di andata e ritorno ...
*beel-**yeht**-toh dee ahn-**dah**-tah eh ree-**tohr**-noh*

... a round trip
... una circolare
... *oo-nah cheer-koh-**lah**-reh*

... first-class, business class
... prima classe, business class
... *pree-mah **klahs**-seh, business class*

Is everything included?
È tutto incluso?
*eh **too**-toh een-**kloo**-soh*

Can you recommend ...?
Potrebbe raccomandare ...?
*poh-**trehb**-beh rahk-koh-mahn-**dah**-reh ...*

... an excursion
... un'escursione
*... oon-eh-skoor-see-**oh**-neh*

Where does it go from?
Da dove parte?
*dah **doh**-veh **pahr**-teh*

How much is the tour?
Quanto costa la gita?
***kwahn**-toh **koh**-stah lah **jee**-tah*

Is there a reduction for children? *(see page 24)*
C'è uno sconto per bambini?
***cheh oo**-noh **skohn**-toh pehr bahm-**bee**-nee*

At what time (does it start)?
A che ora (comincia)?
*ah keh **oh**-rah (koh-**meen**-chah)*

... will it be back?
... sarà di ritorno?
*... sah-**rah** dee ree-**tohr**-noh*

I'd like a sightseeing tour
Vorrei una gita panoramica
vohr-reh-ee oo-nah jee-tah
pah-noh-rah-mee-kah

Will the coach call at the ... hotel?
Si ferma all'albergo ... la corriera?
see fehr-mah ahl-lahl-behr-goh ...
lah kohr-ree-eh-rah

Is lunch included?
È incluso il pranzo di mezzogiorno?
eh een-kloo-zoh eel prahn-tsoh dee
mehd-zoh-johr-noh

What is the oldest building?
Qual'è l'edificio più antico?
kwah-leh leh-dee-fee-choh pee-oo ahn-tee-koh

Is ... open on Sundays?
È aperto di Domenica ...?
eh ah-pehr-toh dee Doh-meh-nee-kah ...

At what time does it open (close)?
A che ora apre (chiude)?
ah keh oh-rah ah-preh (kee-oo-deh)

How far is it to ...?
Quanto lontano è da ...?
kwahn-toh lohn-tah-noh eh dah ...

Is there ... (a train)?
C'è ... (un treno)?
cheh ...(oon treh-noh)

... a coach, bus
... una corriera, un autobus
oo-nah kohr-ree-eh-rah, oon ah-oo-toh-boos

How long does it take ...?
Quanto ci si impiega ...?
kwahn-toh chee see eem-pee-eh-gah ...

... by car
... in macchina
... een mahk-kee-nah

Is there a scenic route?
C'è un tragitto panoramico?
cheh oon trah-jeet-toh pah-noh-rah-mee-koh

Is it safe to swim?
È sicuro nuotare?
eh see-koo-roh nwoh-tah-reh

Luxury
Di lusso
*dee **loos**-soh*

first-class
di prima categoria
*dee **pree**-mah kah-teh-goh-**ree**-ah*

second-class
di seconda categoria
*dee se-**kohn**-dah kah-teh-goh-**ree**-ah*

third, fourth class
di terza, di quarta categoria
*dee **tehr**-tsah, dee **kwahr**-tah
kah-teh-goh-**ree**-ah*

motel, country inn
un motel, una locanda
*oon motel, **oo**-nah loh-**kahn**-dah*

pension, youth hostel
una pensione, un ostello della gioventù
***oo**-nah pehn-see-**oh**-neh, oon
oh-**stehl**-loh **dehl**-lah joh-vehn-**too***

I have a reservation ...
Ho una prenotazione ...
oh oo-nah preh-noh-taht-see-oh-neh ...

Here is the confirmation. I'd like a ...
Qui c'è la conferma. Vorrei una ...
kwee cheh lah kohn-fehr-mah. vohr-reh-ee oo-nah

Have you any rooms vacant?
Avete delle stanze (libere)?
ah-veh-teh dehl-leh stan-tseh (lee-beh-reh)

... (a single room) with (balcony)
... (stanza singola) con (balcone)
(stahn-tsah seen-goh-lah) kohn (bahl-koh-neh)

... double room
... camera doppia
... kah-meh-rah dohp-pee-ah

... with a double bed
... con letto matrimoniale
... kohn-leht-toh mah-tree-moh-nee-ah-leh

... with twin beds, family
... a due letti, per la famiglia
ah doo-eh leht-tee, pehr lah fah-mee-ly-ah

114

... **(without) bath, shower**
... (senza) bagno, doccia
... *(**sehn**-tsah) **bahn**-yoh, **dohch**-cha*

... **toilet, running water**
... gabinetto, acqua corrente
*gah-bee-**neht**-toh, **ahk**-kwah kohr-**rehn**-teh*

Is there (air conditioning)?
C'è (l'aria condizionata)?
***cheh** (**lah**-ree-ah kohn-dee-tsee-oh-**nah**-tah)*

... **heating**
... il riscaldamento
... *eel ree-skahl-dah-**mehn**-toh*

... **radio, television**
... la radio, la televisione
*lah **rahd**-ee-oh, lah teh-leh-vee-zee-**oh**-neh*

... **cable tv, Sky Channel**
... il tele-cavo, lo sky channel
... ***eel** teh-leh-**kah**-voh, **loh** sky **chan**nel*

... **fax machine, computer facilities**
... un fax, un computer
... ***oon fahx, oon** kohm-pee-**oo**-tehr*

I'd like to make ...
Vorrei fare ...
*vohr-**reh**-ee **fah**-reh ...*

... a reservation ...
... una prenotazione ...
... ***oo**-nah preh-noh-tah-tsee-**oh**-neh ...*

... just for tonight
... solo per stanotte
... ***soh**-loh **pehr** stah-**noht**-teh*

... for (two), three, four nights
... per due, tre, quattro notti
... *pehr **doo**-eh, **treh, kwaht**-troh **noht**-tee*

Please show me ...
Per favore mi mostri ...
***pehr** fah-**voh**-reh, mee **moh**-stree ...*

... the calendar
... il calendario
... ***eel** kah-lehn-**dah**-ree-oh*

It must be (quiet) ...
Deve essere tranquilla ...
***deh**-veh **ehs**-seh-reh trahn-**kweel**-lah ...*

... facing the sea
... sul mare
... *sool mah-reh*

... at the (back), front
... sul retro, di facciata
... *sool reh-troh, dee fah-chah-tah*

How much is it (per night), per person ...?
Quanto è (a notte), per persona ...?
kwahn-toh eh (ah noht-teh), pehr per-soh-nah

... at the weekly rate
... a retta settimanale
... *ah reht-tah seht-tee-mah-nah-leh*

... (half) pension (full)
... a (mezza) pensione (pensione completa)
ah (mehts-tsah) pehn-see-oh-ne (kohm-pleh-tah)

Is there (a restaurant)?
C'è il ristorante?
cheh oon ree-stoh-rahn-teh

... room service
... il servizio camere
... *eel sehr-vee-tsee-oh kah-meh-reh*

Here is my passport
Ecco il mio passaporto
*ehk-koh eel **mee**-oh pahs-sah-**pohr**-toh*

Can I pay by Eurocheque?
Posso pagare con un Eurocheque?
pohs**-soh pah-**gah**-reh **kohn oon** eh-oo-roh-**chek

This is all I have
Questo è tutto
***kweh**-stoh **eh toot**-toh*

My luggage is in the car
Il mio bagaglio è in macchina
*eel **mee**-oh bah-**gah**-ly-oh **eh** een **mahk**-kee-nah*

Can you suggest ...?
Potrebbe suggerire ...?
*poh-**trehb**-beh sooj-jeh-**ree**-reh ...*

... another hotel
... un altro albergo
*... oon **ahl**-troh ahl-**berh**-goh*

... a restaurant nearby
... un ristorante qui vicino?
*... oon ree-stoh-**rahn**-teh **kwee** vee-**chee**-noh*

Dear Sirs,
I should like to book a (single, double,
twin) room with (without) (bath, shower,
toilet, running water, balcony, [sea]
view) from (date) until (date) inclusive.
Please can you confirm the booking and
the price (on the following fax number)
(to the above address) by return of post.
Thank you for your help.
Yours faithfully

Cari Signori,
Vorrei prenotare una camera (singola,
matrimoniale, doppia) con (senza)
(bagno, doccia, gabinetto, acqua
corrente, balcone, vista [sul mare]) dal
(...) al (...) incluso. Vi prego di
confermare la prenotazione e il prezzo
(al seguente numero di fax)
(all'indirizzo di cui sopra) a giro di
posta.
Vi ringrazio per l'aiuto.
Distinti saluti

Is there (a camp site) near here?
C'è (un campeggio) qui vicino?
*cheh (oon kahm-**peh**-joh) kwee vee-**chee**-noh*

Is this an authorised ...?
È questo ... autorizzato?
*eh kweh-stoh... ou-toh-ree-**tsah**-toh*

May we ...?
Possiamo ...?
*pohs-see-**ah**-moh ...*

... put up a tent here?
... montare la tenda qui?
*... mohn-**tah**-reh lah **tehn**-dah **kwee***

... park our caravan here?
... parcheggiare qui la nostra roulotte?
*pahr-keh-**jah**-reh **kwee** lah **noh**-strah roo-**loht***

... light a fire?
... accendere un fuoco?
*...ahch-**chen**-deh-reh oon **fwoh**-koh*

... hire a tent?
... noleggiare una tenda?
*... noh-le-**jah**-reh **oo**-nah **tehn**-dah*

What is the hire charge ...?
Quanto costa noleggiare ...?
kwahn-toh koh-stah noh-leh-jah-reh ...

... for (a tent), caravan?
... (una tenda), una roulotte?
... (oo-nah tehn-dah), oo-nah roo-loht

How much ... per person?
Quanto per persona?
kwahn-toh pehr pehr-soh-nah

... per day, per week
... al giorno, alla settimana
... ahl johr-noh, ahl-lah seht-tee-mah-nah

Is the tourist tax included?
È inclusa la tassa turistica?
eh een-kloo-zah lah tahs-sah too-ree-stee-kah

Are there (toilets) ...?
Ci sono dei gabinetti?
chee soh-noh deh-ee gah-bee-neht-tee

... showers
... delle doccie
... dekl-leh dohch-cheh

Is there drinking water?
C'è acqua potabile?
cheh ak-kwah poh-tah-bee-leh

Is there a shop (on the site)?
C'è un negozio (in zona)?
cheh oon neh-goh-tsee-oh (een dzoh-nah)

Where can I buy ...?
Dove si può comprare ...?
doh-veh see pwoh kohm-prah-reh ...

... (paraffin), butane gas
... (paraffina), gas butano
... (pah-rahf-fee-nah), gahz boo-tah-noh

How far is it to the village?
Quanto dista il villaggio?
kwan-toh dees-tah eel vee-lad-joh

... the youth hostel
... l'ostello della gioventù
... loh-stehl-loh dehl-lah joh-nehn-too

Is there a short cut?
C'è una scorciatoia?
cheh oo-nah skor-cha-toh-ee-ah

There is no (soap)
Manca (il sapone)
mahn-kah (eel sah-poh-neh)

... toilet paper
... la carta igienica
... lah kahr-tah ee-jeh-nee-kah

... hot / cold water
...l'acqua calda / fredda
...lahk-kwah kahl-dah / frehd-dah

The washbasin is blocked
Il lavabo è intasato
eel lah-vah-boh eh een-tah-zah-toh

There are no towels
Non ci sono asciugamani
nohn chee soh-noh ah-shoo-gah-mah-nee

These sheets are dirty
Queste lenzuola sono sporche
kweh-stah lehnt-swoh-lah soh-noh spohr-keh

The window is jammed
La finestra è incastrata
lah fee-neh-strah eh een-kah-strah-tah

The toilet won't flush
Lo sciacquone non funziona
*loh shah-**kwoh**-neh nohn foon-tsee-**oh**-nah*

The bulb is burned out
La lampadina è bruciata
*lah lahm-pah-**dee**-nah **eh** broo-**chah**-tah*

The curtains are stuck
Le tende sono incastrate
*leh **tehn**-deh **soh**-noh een-kah-**strah**-teh*

May I have ...?
Potrei aver ...?
*poh-**treh**-ee ah-**veh**-reh ...*

... more hangers?
... qualche altro attaccapanni?
***kwahl**-keh **ahl**-troh aht-tahk-kah-**pahn**-nee*

... another blanket?
... un'altra coperta?
*... oo-**nahl**-trah koh-**pehr**-tah*

... another pillow?
... un altro cuscino?
*... oo-**nahl**-troh koo-**shee**-noh*

Can the ... be turned off?
Si potrebbe chiudere ...?
*see poh-**trehb**-beh chee-**oo**-deh-reh ...*

Can the ... be turned down?
Si potrebbe abbassare ...?
*see poh-**trehb**-beh ahb-bahs-**sah**-reh ...*

... heating
... il riscaldamento
... *eel ree-skahl-dah-**mehn**-toh*

... air conditioning
... l'aria conduizionata
... ***lah**-ree-ah kohn-dee-tsee-oh-**nah**-tah*

The ... doesn't work
Il... non funziona.
*eel ... **nohn** foon-tsee-**oh**-nah*

... fan ...
... il ventilatore ...
... *eel veh-ntee-lah-**toh**-reh ...*

... shaver point ...
... presa per il rasoio elettrico ...
***preh**-sah pehr eel rah-**soh**-ee-oh eh-**leht**-tree-koh*

Is the hotel open all night?
È aperto tutta la notte l'albergo?
*eh ah-**pehr**-toh **toot**-tah lah **noht**-teh lal-**behr**-goh*

When does it close?
A che ora chiude?
*ah keh **oh**-rah kee-**oo**-deh*

Is there a garage (parking)?
C'è un garage (un parcheggio)?
***cheh** oon gah-**rahj** (oon pahr-**kehj**-joh)*

Where is the ... (dining room)?
Dov'è ... (la sala da pranzo)?
*doh-**veh** ... (lah **sah**-lah dah **prahn**-tsoh)*

... bathroom, emergency exit
... bagno, uscita di emergenza
***bahn**-yoh, oo-**shee**-tah dee eh-mehr-**jehn**-tsah*

My key, please
La mia chiave, per favore
*lah **mee**-ah kee-**ah**-veh, pehr fah-**voh**-reh*

What's the voltage?
Quant'è il voltaggio?
*kwahn-**teh** eel vohl-**tahj**-joh*

At what time is ... (breakfast)?
A che ora è ... (la colazione)?
*ıh keh **oh**-rah **eh** ...(lah koh-lah-tsee-**oh**-neh)*

Can we have ... ?
Possiamo avere un ... ?
*vohs-see-**ah**-moh ah-**veh**-reh oon ...*

... lunch, dinner ...
... pranzo, cena ...
*.. **prahn**-tsoh, **cheh**-nah ...*

.. in our room
... nella nostra stanza
*.. **nehl**-lah **noh**-strah **stahn**-tsah*

Please wake me at ... *(see page 18 for time)*
Per favore, mi svegli alle ...
*vehr fah-**voh**-reh, mee **zvehl**-yee **ahl**-leh ...*

I'd like to leave this ...
Vorrei lasciare questo ...
*vohr-**reh**-ee lah-**shah**-reh **kweh**-stoh ...*

.. in your safe
.. nella vostra cassaforte
*.. **nehl**-lah **voh**-strah kahs-sah-**fohr**-teh*

Are there any messages for me?
Ci sono messaggi per me?
*chee **soh**-noh mehs-**sahj**-ee pehr meh*

Can you find me a ...?
Mi potrebbe trovare un ...?
*mee poh-**trehb**-beh troh-**vah**-reh oon ...*

... babysitter
... una babysitter
*... **oo**-nah beh-bee-**seet**-tehr*

... iron
... un ferro da stiro
*... oon **fehr**-roh dah **stee**-roh*

... computer
... un computer
*... oon kohm-pee-**oo**-tehr*

Could you put a cot ...?
Potrebbe mettere una branda ...?
*poh-**trehb**-beh **meht**-theh-reh **oo**-nah **brahn**-dah*

... in the room
... nella stanza
*... **nehl**-lah **stahn**-tsah*

128

I'd like ... in my room
Vorrei ... in camera
*vohr-**reh**-ee ... een **kah**-meh-rah*

... breakfast ...
... la colazione ...
... *lah koh-laht-see-**oh**-neh* ...

...lunch, dinner, a snack ...
... pranzo, cena, uno spuntino ...
... ***prahn**-tsoh, **cheh**-nah, **oo**-noh spoon-**tee**-noh*

May I see the ... please?
Potrei vedere il ... per favore?
*poh-**treh**-ee veh-**deh**-reh eel ... pehr fah-**voh**-reh*

.. menu ...
.. menù ...
.. *meh-**noo*** ...

.. wine list ...
.. la lista dei vini ...
.. *lah **lee**-stah **deh**-ee **vee**-nee* ...

Is there a set menu?
C'è un menù fisso?
*cheh oon meh-**noo** **fees**-soh*

129

Do you serve local dishes?
Servite piatti locali?
*sehr-**vee**-teh pee-**aht**-tee loh-**kah**-lee*

I just want ...
Vorrei solo ...
*vohr-**reh**-ee **soh**-loh ...*

... something light
... qualcosa di leggero
*... kwahl-**koh**-zah dee lehj-**jeh**-roh*

... (without fat, oil, salt)
... (senza grasso, olio, sale)
*... (**sehn**-tsah **grahs**-soh, **ohl**-yoh, **sah**-leh)*

I'm ... (on a diet)
Sono ... (a dieta)
***soh**-noh ... (ah dee-**eh**-tah)*

... vegetarian
... vegetariano
*... veh-jeh-tah-ree-**ah**-noh*

... a diabetic
... sono diabetico
*... **soh**-noh dee-ah-**beh**-tee-koh*

Can I walk to ...?
Si può andare a piedi fino ...?
*see **pwoh** ahn-**dah**-reh ah pee-**eh**-dee **fee**-noh*

... the shops?
... al negozio?
*... ahl neh-**goht**-see-oh*

How long does it take?
Quanto ci si impiega?
*kwahn-toh **chee** see eem-pee-**eh**-gah*

How far is it?
Quanto lontano è?
kwahn**-toh lohn-**tah**-noh **eh

Is there a market nearby?
C'è un mercato qui vicino?
***cheh** oon mehr-**kah**-toh **kwee** vee-**chee**-noh*

Can I buy ... there?
Si può comprare ... là?
*see **pwoh** kohm-**prah**-reh ... **lah***

... fresh bread ...
... pane fresco ...
*... **pah**-neh **freh**-skoh ...*

131

May I help myself?
Posso servirmi da solo?
pohs-soh sehr-***veer***-mee dah ***soh***-loh

I'd like (6 eggs) ...
Vorrei sei uova ...
*vohr-**reh**-ee **seh**-ee **woh**-vah ...*

... a litre of milk
... un litro di latte
... *oon **lee**-troh dee **laht**-teh*

... some bread, cheese
... un po' di pane, del formaggio
... *oon poh dee **pah**-neh, dehl fohr-**maj**-joh*

... a (half) kilo of ...
... (mezzo) chilo di ...
... *(**mehd**-zoh) **kee**-loh dee ...*

... fish, fruit, meat, vegetables
... pesce, frutta, carne, verdure
... *peh-sheh, **froot**-tah, **kahr**-neh, vehr-**doo**-reh*

... apples, onions
... mele, cipolle
... *meh-leh, chee-**pohl**-leh*

... **potatoes, tomatoes**
... patate, pomidoro
... *pah-**tah**-teh, poh-meeh-**doh**-roh*

... **100 grammes of ...**
... 100 grammi di ...
... ***chehn**-toh **grahm**-mee dee ...*

... **butter, garlic**
... burro, aglio
... ***boor**-roh, **ahl**-yoh*

... **2, 4, 6 slices ...**
... due, quattro, sei fette di ...
... ***doo**-eh, **kwaht**-troh, **seh**-ee **feht**-teh dee*

... **cooked ham**
... prosciutto cotto
... *proh-**shoot**-toh **koht**-toh*

I'll have one of those
Vorrei avere uno di quelli
*vohr-**reh**-ee ah-**veh**-reh **oo**-noh dee **kwehl**-lee*

What sort of cheese is that?
Che tipo di formaggio è quello?
*keh **tee**-poh dee fohr-**mahj**-joh **eh kwehl**-loh*

I'm leaving early in the morning
Parto la mattina presto
pahr-toh lah maht-tee-nah preh-stoh

We'll be leaving around midday
Partiremo verso mezzogiorno
pahr-tee-reh-moh vehr-soh mehd-zoh-johr-noh

I must go right away
Devo partire subito
De-voh pahr-tee-reh soo-bee-toh

Can you make up my bill?
Potrebbe prepararmi il conto?
poh-trehb-beh preh-pah-rahr-mee eel kohn-toh

Is everything included?
È tutto incluso?
eh too-toh een-kloo-zoh

What is this amount for?
Per che cos'è questa somma?
pehr keh koh-zeh kweh-stah sohm-mah

Thank you for a very pleasant stay
Grazie per l'ottimo soggiorno
grah-tsee-eh pehr loht-tee-moh sohj-johr-noh

Where's the nearest ... (bank)?
Dov'è ... (la banca) più vicina?
*dohv-**eh** (lah **bahn**-kah) pee-**oo** veh-**chee**-nah*

... currency exchange office
... ufficio di cambio valuta
... *oof-**fee**-choh dee **kahm**-bee-oh vah-**loo**-tah*

I want to change ...
Vorrei cambiare ...
*vohr-**reh**-ee kahm-bee-**ah**-reh ...*

... some pounds, dollars
... delle sterline, dei dollari
... ***dehl**-leh stehr-**lee**-neh, **deh**-ee **dohl**-lah-ree*

Do you change ... (travellers' cheques)?
Cambiate ... (travellers cheques)?
*kahm-bee-**ah**-teh ... (**trah**-vehl-lers-chehks)*

... Eurocheques
... Eurocheques
... *eh-**oo**-roh-chehks*

I have a credit card
Ho una carta di credito
***oh** oo-nah **kahr**-tah dee **kreh**-dee-toh*

What's ... (the exchange rate) for ...?
Quant'è ... (il tasso di scambio) per ...?
kwahn-teh ... (eel tahs-soh dee skahm-bee-oh) pehr

... your commission
... la sua commissione
... *lah soo-ah kohm-mees-see-oh-neh*

Can you give me ... ?
Potrebbe darmi ... ?
poh-trehb-beh dahr-mee ...

... notes, some change
... delle banconote, delle monete
dehl-leh bahn-koh-noh-teh, dehl-leh moh-neh-teh

Will you take ...?
Accettate ...?
ah-cheht-tah-teh ...

... a personal cheque
... un assegno personale
... *oon ahs-sehn-yoh pehr-soh-nah-leh*

... this credit card
... questa carta di credito
... *kweh-stah kahr-tah dee kreh-dee-toh*

I'm expecting ... (some money) ... from ...
Aspetto ... (un po' di soldi) ... da ...
*ah-**speht**-toh ... (oon **poh** dee **sohl**-dee) ... dah*

... letter of credit ...
... la lettera di credito ...
... *lah **leht**-teh-rah dee **kreh**-dee-toh ...*

... Australia, Canada
... l'Australia, il Canada
... *l'ou-**strah**-lee-ah, eel **kah**-nah-dah*

... New Zealand
... la Nuova Zelanda
... *lah noo-**oh**-vah dzeh-**lahn**-dah*

... UK
... il Regno Unito
... *eel **rehn**-yoh oo-**nee**-toh*

... USA
... gli Stati Uniti D'America
*lyee **stah**-tee oo-**nee**-tee dahh-**meh**-ree-kah*

Has it arrived?
È arrivato?
*eh ahr-ree-**vah**-toh*

In Italy there is a clear distinction between pharmacy *(farmacia)* and perfumery *(profumeria)*. In *farmacia* you can only get medicines and drugs on prescription. In *profumeria* you can get only perfumes, cosmetics, and soaps.

In a FARMACIA

Where's the nearest ...?
Dov'è la più vicina ...?
*dohv-**eh**lahpee-**oo**vee-**chee**-nah...*

... (all-night) chemist
... farmacia (notturna)
*... fahr-mah-**chee**-ah (noht-**toor**-nah)*

baby needs
articoli per il bebè
*ahr-**tee**-koh-lee **pehr** eel beh-**beh***

I would like ... (some baby food)
Vorrei (degli omogeneizzati)
*vohr-**reh**-ee (**deh**-ly oh-moh-jeh-neh-ee-**tsah**-tee)*

... a dummy
... un succhiotto
*oon sook-kee-**oht**-toh*

... a feeding bottle
... un biberon
*oon bee-beh-**rohn***

... some nappies
... dei pannolini
*deh-ee pahn-nohh-**lee**-nee*

Can you make up this ...?
Potrebbe prepararmi questa ...?
*poh-**trehb**-beh preh-pah-**rahr**-mee **kweh**-stah*

Can I get this ...?
Posso prendere questo ...?
***pohs**-soh **prehn**-deh-reh **kweh**-stoh ...*

... (without a) prescription
... (senza) ricetta
*... (**sehn**-tsah) ree-**cheht**-tah*

Can you give me something for ...?
Potrebbe darmi qualcosa per ...?
*poh-**trehb**-beh **dahr**-mee kwahl-**koh**-sah pehr*

... cold, colic
... reffreddore, coliche
... *rahf-frehd-**doh**-reh, **koh**-lee-keh*

... constipation, diarrhoea
... stitichezza, diarrea
... *stee-tee-**keht**-tsah, dee-ahr-**reh**-ah*

... cough, fever, 'flu
... tosse, febbre, influenza
... ***tohs**-seh, **fehb**-breh, een-floo-**ehn**-tsah*

... indigestion
... indigestione
... *een-dee-jeh-stee-**oh**-neh*

... insomnia, headache
... insonnia, mal di testa
... *een-**sohn**-nee-ah, **mahl** dee **teh**-sta*

... insect bites
... punture di insetti
... *poon-**too**-reh dee een-**seht**-tee*

... stomach-ache (upper) / lower stomach
... mal di (stomaco) / pancia
... *mahl dee (stoh-mah-koh) / **pahn**-chah*

... sunburn
... scottature solari
... *skoht-tah-**too**-reh soh-**lah**-ree*

... (travel), sea sickness
... mal (di macchina), di mare
... ***mahl** (dee **mahk**-kee-nah), dee **mah**-reh*

... upset stomach / nausea / vomiting
... mal di stomaco / nausea / vomito
***mahl** dee **stoh**-mah-koh / **nah**-oo-seh-ah / **voh**-mee-toh*

I would like one (two, three) ...
Vorrei un (due, tre) ...
*vohr-**reh**-ee oon (doo-eh, treh) ...*

... packet/s of condoms
... pacchetto/i di preservativi
*pahk-**keht**-toh/tee **dee** preh-sehr-vah-**tee**-vee*

... press-on towels
... assorbenti igienici
... *ahs-sohr-**behn**-tee ee-**jeh**-nee-chee*

... tampons (Tampax, O.B.)
... tamponi (Tampax, O-Bi)
... *tahm-**poh**-nee (**tahm**-pax, **oh**-bee)*

In a PROFUMERIA

toiletries (articoli da toilette)

a blusher, a foundation
un rouge, un fondotinta
oon roo-jeh, oon fohn-doh-teen-tah

a cleansing lotion
un latte detergente
oon laht-teh deh-tehr-jehn-teh

a comb
un pettine
oon peht-tee-neh

conditioner (shampoo) for ...
del balsamo (dello shampoo) per ...
dehl bahl-sah-moh (dehl-loh sham-poh) pehr

... dry (oily) hair
... secchi (grassi) capelli
... sehk-kee (grahs-see) kah-pehl-lee

... hair with dandruff / normal
... capelli con forfora / normali
kah-pehl-lee kohn fohr-foh-rah / nohr-mah-lee

cotton wool
del cotone idrofilo
*dehl koh-**toh**-neh ee-**droh**-fee-loh*

a day cream
una crema diurna
*oo-nah **kreh**-mah dee-oor-nah*

deodorant
del deodorante
*dehl deh-oh-doh-**rahn**-teh*

emery board
una limetta da unghie
*oo-nah lee-**meht**-tah dah **oon**-gee-eh*

an eyeshadow, a mascara
un ombretto, un mascara
*oon ohm-**breht**-toh, **oon** mah-**skah**-rah*

a hairbrush
una spazzola da capelli
*oo-nah **spah**-tsoh-lah dah kah-**pehl**-lee*

a hair dye
una tinta per capelli
*oo-nah **teen**-tah pehr kah-**pehl**-lee*

lip salve
del burro di cacao
dehl boor-roh dee kah-kah-oh

a lipstick
un rossetto
oon rohs-seht-toh

moisturising cream
una crema emolliente
oo-nah kreh-mah eh-mohl-lee-ehn-teh

a nail varnish
uno smalto per unghie
oo-noh smahl-toh dah oon-gee-eh

some razor blades
delle lamette da barba
dehl-leh lah-meht-teh dah bahr-bah

a razor, shaving cream
un rasoio, della crema da barba
oon rah-zoh-ee-oh, dehl-lah creh-mah dah bahr-bah

a shaving brush
un pennello da barba
oon pehn-nehl-loh dah bahr-bah

sun cream
una crema solare
oo-nah **creh**-*mah soh-**lah**-reh*

talcum powder
del borotalco
dehl *boh-roh-**tahl**-koh*

tissues
dei fazzoletti di carta
*deh-ee fah-tsoh-**leht**-tee dee **kahr**-tah*

toilet paper
della carta igienica
*dehl-lah **kahr**-tah ee-**jeh**-nee-kah*

a toothbrush
uno spazzolino da denti
*oo-noh spah-tsoh-**lee**-noh dah dehn-tee*

toothpaste
del dentifricio
*dehl dehn-tee-**free**-choo*

tweezers
una pinzetta
*oo-nah peen-**tseht**-tah*

145

Where is the nearest ...?
Dov'è la ... più vicina?
*doh-**veh** lah ... pee-**oo** vee-**chee**-nah*

... laundry, dry cleaner
... lavanderia, pulisecco ...
*... lah-vahn-deh-**ree**-ah, poo-lee-**sehk**-koh*

I'd like these clothes ...
Vorrei pulire questi vestiti ...
*vohr-**reh**-ee poo-**lee**-reh **kweh**-stee veh-**stee**-tee*

... to be cleaned, pressed, washed
... da pulire, stirare, lavare
*... dah poo-**lee**-reh, stee-**rah**-reh, lah-**vah**-reh*

Can you deliver them?
Potrebbe farli recapitare?
*poh-**trehb**-beh fahr-**lee** reh-kak-pee-**tah**-reh*

There's a hole in this
C'è un buco in questo
***cheh** oon **boo**-koh een **kweh**-stoh*

Do you do invisible mending?
Fate rammendi invisibili?
***fah**-teh rahm-**mehn**-dee een-vee-**zee**-bee-lee*

Can you get out ...?
È possibile togliere ...?
*eh pohs-**see**-bee-leh **tohl**-yeh-reh ...*

... this stain
... questa macchia
... ***kweh**-stah **mahk**-kee-ah*

... it's coffee, fruit juice
... è caffè, succo di frutta
... *eh kahf-**eh**, **sook**-koh dee **froot**-tah*

... grease, wine
... grasso, vino
... ***grahs**-soh, **vee**-noh*

When will they be ready?
Quando saranno pronti?
***kwahn**-doh sah-**rahn**-noh **prohn**-tee*

I need them by ... (tonight)
Ne ho bisogno per ... (stasera)
*neh **oh** bee-**sohn**-yoh pehr ... (stah-**seh**-rah)*

... tomorrow, before ...
... domani, prima ...
... *doh-**mah**-nee, **pree**-mah ...*

Is my laundry ready?
È pronto il mio bucato?
*eh **prohn**-toh eel **mee**-oh boo-**kah**-toh*

This isn't mine
Questo non è mio
*kweh-stoh nohn **eh mee**-oh*

There's (something) a button missing
Manca (qualcosa) un bottone
***mahn**-kah (kwahl-**koh**-zah) oon boht-**toh**-neh*

Can you sew on ...?
Potrebbe cucire ...?
*poh-**trehb**-beh koo-**chee**-reh ...*

... this button?
... questo bottone?
*... **kweh**-stoh boht-**toh**-neh*

Can I pay ...?
Posso pagare ...?
***pohs**-soh pah-**gah**-reh ...*

... with this credit card
... con questa carta di credito
*... kohn **kweh**-stah **kahr**-tah dee **creh**-dee-toh*

I want something for ...
Vorrei qualcosa per ...
*vohr-**reh**-ee kwahl-**koh**-sah pehr ...*

... a boy / girl
... un bambino / una bambina
*... oon bahm-**bee**-noh / oo-nah bahm-**bee**-nah*

... a ten-year-old
... di dieci anni
*... dee dee-**eh**-chee **ahn**-nee*

... him / her ...
... lui / lei ...
*... **loo**-ee / **leh**-ee ...*

... to match this
... per accompagnarlo a questo
*... pehr ahk-kohm-pahn-**yahr**-loh ah **kweh**-stoh*

... the same colour as this
... dello stesso colore di questo
*... **dehl**-loh **stehs**-soh koh-**loh**-reh dee **kweh**-stoh*

I like (the one in the window)
Mi piace (quello in vetrina)
*mee pee-**ah**-cheh (**kwehl**-loh een veh-**tree**-nah)*

I'd like something ...
Vorrei qualcosa ...
vohr-reh-ee kwahl-koh-sah ...

... darker, lighter
... più scuro, più chiaro
... pee-oo skoo-roh, pee-oo kee-ah-roh

... thicker, thinner
... più grosso, più sottile
... pee-oo grohs-soh, pee-oo soht-tee-leh

Have you anything in ...
Avrebbe qualcosa in ...
ah-vrehb-beh kwahl-koh-zah een ...

... wool, cotton
... di lana, di cotone
... dee lah-nah, dee koh-toh-neh

... silk, leather
... di seta, di pelle (di cuoio)
... dee seh-tah, dee pehl-leh (dee kwoh-ee-oh)

Where's the fitting room?
C'è un camerino?
cheh oon kah-meh-ree-noh

It's too ... (long)
È troppo ... (lungo)
eh trohp-poh ... (loon-goh)

... short, loose, tight
... corto, abbondante, attillato
kohr-toh, ahb-bohn-dahn-teh, aht-tee-lah-toh

It's too expensive for me
È troppo caro per me
eh trohp-poh kah-roh pehr meh

I don't know Italian sizes *(see page 153)*
Non conosco le taglie italiane
nohn ko-noh-skoh leh tahl-yeh ee-tah-lee-ah-neh

Do you have the same in ...?
Ha lo stesso in ...?
ah loh stehs-soh een ...

... almost black, black, blue
... nerastro, nero, azzurro
... neh-rah-stroh, neh-roh, ah-dzoor-roh

... light blue, dark (jeans) blue, turquoise
... celeste, blu, turchese
... cheh-leh-steh, bloo, toor-keh-zeh

... beige, light brown, brown
... beige, marroncino, marrone
... *beh*-j, *mahr-rohn-chee-noh, mahr-roh-neh*

... dark green, light green, green
... verdone, verdino, verde
... *vehr-doh-neh, vehr-dee-noh, vehr-deh*

... (emerald), pea-green
... verde (smeraldo), pisello
... *vehr-deh (smeh-rahl-doh), pee-zehl-loh*

... grey, orange, yellow
... grigio, arancione, giallo
... *gree-joh, ah-rahn-choh-neh, jahl-loh*

... indigo, light violet, purple
... indaco, violetto, porpora
... *een-dah-koh, vee-oh-leht-toh, pohr-poh-rah*

... pink, violet, wine red, white
... rosa, viola, Bordeaux, bianco
... *roh-sah, vee-oh-lah, bohr-doh, bee-ahn-koh*

... (scarlet) red, clay-, purple-, red
... rosso (scarlatto), argilla, porpora
rohs-soh (scahr-laht-toh), ahr-jeel-la, pohr-poh-rah

Women – dresses, suits

UK	8	10	12	14	16	18	20	22	24	26
Eur	34	36	38	40	42	44	46	48	50	52

Men – suits, overcoats

UK	36	38	40	42	44	46	48	50	52
Eur	46	48	50	52	54	56	58	60	62

Women – stockings

UK	8	8½	9	9½	10	10½
Eur	0	1	2	3	4	5

and shoes

UK	4½	5	5½	6	6½	7	7½
Eur	37	38	39	39/40	40	41	41/42

Men – shoes

UK	6	7	8	8½	9	9½	10	10½	11
Eur	39	41	42	43	43	44	45	46	46

Men – shirts

UK	14	14½	15	15½	16	16½	17	17½	18
Eur	36	37	38	39	41	42	43	44	45

I'd like to buy a gift ...
Vorrei fare un regalo ...
vohr-reh-ee fahr-eh oon reh-gah-loh ...

... for ... (my father), my mother
... a ... (mio papà), mia mamma
ah ... (mee-oh pah-pah), mee-ah mahm-mah

... my grandfather, my grandmother
... mio nonno, mia nonna
... mee-oh nohn-noh, mee-ah nohn-nah

... my (daughter), sister, girlfriend
... mia (figlia), sorella, ragazza
... mee-ah feel-yah, soh-rehl-lah, rah-gaht-tsah

... my (brother), son, boyfriend
... mio (fratello), figlio, ragazzo
... mee-oh (frah-tehl-loh), feel-yoh, rah-gaht-tsoh

... my wife, my husband
... mia moglie, mio marito
... mee-ah mohl-yeh, mee-oh mah-ree-toh

... my fiancé / e
... mio / mia fidanzato / a
... mee-oh / mee-ah fee-dahn-tsah-toh / tah

... for a friend (male / female)
... a' un amico / amica
... *ah oon ah-**mee**-koh / ah-**mee**-ah*

He / she likes ...
A lui / lei piacciono ...
*ah **loo**-ee / **leh**-ee pee-**ah**-choh-noh ...*

... antiques, ceramics
... l'antiquariato, le ceramiche
*lahn-tee-kwah-ree-**ah**-toh, leh che-**rah**-mee-keh*

... Bassano ceramics
... le ceramiche di Bassano
... *leh che-**rah**-mee-keh dee Bahs-**sah**-noh*

... chocolate, cooking
... la cioccolata, la cucina
... *lah chok-koh-**lah**-tah, lah koo-**chee**-nah*

... the local cakes, pasta
... i dolci locali, la pasta
... *ee **dohl**-chee loh-**kah**-lee, lah **pahs**-ta*

... the local olive oil
... l'olio d'oliva locale
... ***loh**-lee-oh doh-**lee**-vah loh-**kah**-leh*

... the local salami
... i salumi locali
... *ee sah-**loo**-mee loh-**kah**-lee*

... Parma hams
... i prosciutti di Parma
... *ee proh-**shoot**-tee dee **pahr**-mah*

... Parmesan cheese
... il Parmigiano
... *eel pahr-mee-**jah**-noh*

... glass, jewellery
... il vetro, i gioielli
... *eel **veh**-troh, ee joh-ee-**ehl**-lee*

... Burano glass
... i vetri di Burano
... *ee **veh**-tree dee boo-**rah**-noh*

... goldcraft
... l'oreficeria
... *loh-reh-fee-cheh-**ree**-ah*

... footwear
... le calzature
... *leh kal-tsah-**too**-reh*

... **knitwear**
... gli articoli di maglia
... *lyee ahr-**tee**-koh-lee dee **mah**-lyah*

... **leatherwear**
... gli articoli in pelle
... *ly ahr-**tee**-koh-lee een **pehl**-leh*

... **the local handicraft**
... l'artigianato locale
... *lahr-tee-jah-**nah**-toh loh-**kah**-leh*

... **needlework, silver**
... i ricami, l'argenteria
... *ee ree-**kah**-mee, lahr-jehn-teh-**ree**-ah*

... **woodwork, wine**
... i lavori di intaglio, i vini
... *ee lah-**voh**-ree dee een-**tahl**-yoh, ee **vee**-nee*

... **local wines**
... i vini locali
... *ee **vee**-nee loh-**kah**-lee*

... **(red, white, rosé)**
... (i rossi, bianchi, i rosé)
... *(ee **rohs**-see, ee bee-**ahn**-kee, ee roh-**seh**)*

Where's the (best) ...?
Dov'è il (migliore) ...
*dohv-**eh** eel (meel-**yoh**-reh)* ...

... (nearest)
... più vicino?
*... pee-**oo** vee-**chee**-noh*

... barber, hairdresser
... barbiere, parrucchiere ...
*... bahr-bee-**eh**-reh, pahr-rook-kee-**eh**-reh* ...

Can I make ...?
Posso fissare ...?
***pohs**-so fees-**sah**-reh* ...

... an appointment for ... *(see pages 15-20)*
... un appuntamento per ...
*... oon ahp-poon-tah-**mehn**-toh pehr* ...

I'd like a haircut
Vorrei un taglio di capelli
*vohr-**reh**-ee oon **tah**-lyoh dee kah-**pehl**-lee*

I want it cut ...
Vorrei taglio ...
*vohr-**reh**-ee **tahl**-yoh* ...

... and shaped ...
... e messa in piega ...
... *eh **mehs**-sah een pee-**eh**-gah* ...

... with a fringe
... con la frangia
... *kohn lah **frahn**-jah*

... don't take off too much!
... non tagli troppo!
... *nohn **tahl**-yee **trohp**-poh*

Please use shampoo ...
Per favore usi lo shampoo ...
*pehr fah-**voh**-reh oo-zee loh **shahm**-poo* ...

... anti-dandruff, for dry hair
... anti forfora, per capelli secchi
*ahn-tee **fohr**-foh-rah, pehr kah-pehl-lee **sehk**-kee*

... for (normal), oily hair
... per capelli (normali), grassi
... *pehr kah-pehl-lee (nohr-**mah**-lee), **grahs**-see*

... conditioner, hairspray, gel, foam
... balsamo, lacca, gel, schiuma
... ***bahl**-sah-moh, **lahk**-kah, **jehl**, skee-**oo**-mah*

(The water), the dryer ...
(L'acqua), il casco / il fon ...
*(lahk-kwah), eel **kah**-skoh / **fohn** ...*

... is too (hot), cold
... è troppo (calda/o) fredda/o
*... **eh trohp**-poh (**kahl**-dah/oh) **frehd**-dah/oh*

A little more off ...
Tagli un po' di più...
***tahl**-yee oon poh dee pee-**oo**...*

... of the back, of the neck
... sulla nuca, sul collo
*... sool-lah **noo**-kah, sool **kohl**-loh*

... from the sides, from the top
... ai lati, sopra la testa
*... ah-ee **lah**-tee, **soh**-prah lah **teh**-stah*

Please trim my ...
Per favore, mi aggiusti ...
*pehr fah-**voh**-reh, mee ahj-**joo**-stee ...*

... beard, moustache, sideburns
... la barba, i baffi, le basette
*... lah **bahr**-bah ee **bahf**-fee, leh bah-**seht**-teh*

Please set it ...
La messa in piega, per favore ...
*lah **mehs**-sah een pee-**eh**-gah, pehr fah-**voh**-reh*

... without rollers
... senza bigodini
... ***sehn**-tsah bee-goh-**dee**-nee*

... on (large), small rollers
... su bigodini (larghi), stretti
*... soo bee-goh-**dee**-nee (**lahr**-gee) **sreht**-tee*

... a bit straighter, with highlights
... un po' più dritti, con le mesh
*... oon **poh** pee-**oo dreet**-tee, **kohn** leh **mesh***

... more wavy, more curly
... più ondulati, più ricci
*... pee-**oo** ohn-doo-**lah**-tee, **reec**-chee*

... blond, light blond, brown
... biondo, chiaro, castano
*... bee-**ohn**-doh, kee-**ah**-roh, kah-**stah**-noh*

... dark brown, red, black
... castano scuro, rosso, nero
*... kah-**stah**-noh **skoo**-roh, **rohs**-soh, **neh**-roh*

Have you (a film) ...?
Avrebbe (una pellicola) ...?
*ah-**vrehb**-beh (**oo**-nah pehl-**lee**-koh-lah) ...*

... video cassette
... una video cassetta
*... oo-nah **vee**-deh-oh kahs-**seht**-tah*

... for this camera
... per questa macchina
*... pehr **kweh**-stah **mahk**-kee-nah*

... black and white
... bianco e nero
*... bee-**ahn**-koh eh **neh**-roh*

... colour print
... stampa a colori
*... **stahm**-pah ah koh-**loh**-ree*

... colour negative
... una negativa a colori
*... **oo**-nah neh-gah-**tee**-vah ah koh-**loh**-ree*

... colour slide
... una diapositiva a colori
*oo-nah dee-ah-poh-see-**tee**-vah ah koh-**loh**-ree*

... **for artificial light** ...
... per luce artificiale ...
... *pehr loo-cheh ahr-tee-fee-chah-leh* ...

... **natural light** ...
... per luce naturale ...
... *pehr loo-cheh nah-too-rahl-leh...*

... **fast, slow**
... veloce, lenta
... *veh-loh-che, lehn-tah-h*

... **this ASA (DIN) number**
... questo numero ASA (DIN)
... *kweh-stoh noo-meh-roh ah-sah (deen)*

... **including processing**
... incluso lo sviluppo
... *een-kloo-soh loh zvee-loop-poh*

I'd like this film ...
Vorrei ... questa pellicola
vohr-reh-ee ... kweh-stah pehl-lee-koh-lah

... **developed and printed** ...
... sviluppata e stampata ...
... *svee-loop-pah-tah eh stahm-pah-tah* ...

Please fit the film ...
Per favore mi metta la pellicola ...
*pehr fah-**voh**-reh mee **meht**-tah lah pehl-**lee**-koh-lah*

The film is jammed ...
La pellicola è incastrata ...
*lah pehl-**lee**-koh-lah **eh** een-kah-**strah**-tah ...*

... in the camera
... nella macchina
... ***nehl**-lah **mahk**-kee-nah*

How much for developing ...?
Quanto costa lo sviluppo ...?
***kwahn**-to **koh**-stah loh svee-**oop**-poh ...*

I want ... (a print) ...
Vorrei (stampare) ...
*vohr-**reh**-ee (stahm-**pah**-reh) ...*

... an enlargement ...
... un ingrandimento ...
... *oon een-grahn-dee-**mehn**-toh ...*

... of each negative
... ogni negativa
... ***oh**-ny neh-gah-**tee**-vah*

... with a ... (matte) finish
... con superficie ... (opaca)
... *kon soo-pehr-**fee**-cheh ... (oh-**pah**-kah)*

... glossy
... lucida
... *loo-chee-dah*

When will they be ready?
Quando saranno pronti?
***kwahn**-doh sah-**rahn**-noh **prohn**-tee*

Do you have flash cubes?
Avete ricambi per il flash?
*ah-**veh**-teh ree-**kahm**-bee pehr eel **flahsh***

... bulbs, batteries ...
... lampadine, pile ...
... *lahm-pah-**dee**-neh, **pee**-leh ...*

... like this
... come questa
... ***koh**-meh **kweh**-stah*

How much do I owe you?
Quanto le devo?
***kwahn**-toh leh **deh**-voh*

Where is the post box?
Dov'è la buca delle posta?
*doh-**veh** lah **boo**-kah **dehl**-lah **poh**-stah*

Is there a post office ...?
C'è un ufficio postale ...?
***cheh** oon oof-**fee**-cho poh-**stah**-leh ...*

... near here
... qui vicino
*... **kwee** vee-chee-noh*

Which window ...
A quale sportello ...
*ah **kwah**-leh spohr-**tehl**-loh ...*

... do I go to for ...
... devo andare per ...
*... **deh**-voh ahn-**dah**-reh pehr ...*

... stamps, telegrams
... francobolli, telegrammi
*... frahn-koh-**bohl**-lee, teh-leh-**grahm**-mee*

... money orders
... ordini di denaro
*... **ohr**-dee-nee dee deh-**nah**-roh*

How much ...?
Quanto costa ...?
kwahn-toh koh-stah ...

... for this (letter) ...
... spedire questa (lettera) ...
... speh-dee-reh kweh-stah (leht-teh-rah) ...

... (card) to England
... (cartolina) in Inghilterra
... (kahr-toh-lee-nah) een een-geel-tehr-rah

... to send this package to ...
... mandare questo pacco in...
... mahn-dah-reh kweh-stoh pahk-koh een

... America, Australia
... America, Australia
... ah-meh-ree-kah, ou-strah-lee-ah

... Ireland, New Zealand
... Irlanda, Nuova Zelanda
... eer-lahn-dah, nwoh-vah dzeh-lahn-dah

... Scotland, Wales, Canada
... Scozia, Galles, Canada
... skoht-see-ah, gahl-lehs, kah-nah-dah

... by air mail, express
... per via aerea, espresso
... *pehr **vee**-ah ah-**eh**-re-ah, ehs-**prehs**-soh*

... registered
... raccomandata
... *rah-k-koh-mahn-**dah**-tah*

I want to send a cable
Vorrei mandare un telegramma
*vohr-**reh**-ee mahn-**dah**-reh oon teh-leh-**gram**-mah*

Reply paid, overnight (of telegrams etc)
Risposta pagata, notturno
*ree-**spoh**-stah pah-**gah**-tah, noht-**toor**-noh*

How much is it per word?
Quant'è per parola?
*kwahn-**teh** pehr pah-**roh**-lah*

Can you give me a form?
Potrebbe darmi un modulo?
*poh-**trehb**-beh **dahr**-mee oon **moh**-doo-loh*

Is there any mail for me? I am ...
C'è posta per me? Sono ...
*cheh **poh**-stah pehr meh, **soh**-noh ...*

Call the police ... (telephone 112 or 113)
Chiami la polizia ...
*kee-**ah**-mee lah poh-leet-**see**-ah ...*

... there's been an accident
... c'è stato un incidente
... ***cheh stah**-toh oon een-chee-**dehn**-teh*

My little boy (girl)
Il mio (la mia) bambino(a)
*eel **mee**-oh (lah **mee**-ah) bahm-**bee**-noh-(nah)*

... has hurt (him) herself
... si è fatta male
... *see eh **faht**-tah **mah**-leh*

Call ... (an ambulance), quickly!
Chiami ... (un'ambulanza), presto!
*kee-ah-mee (oon-ahm-boo-**lahn**-tsah), **preh**-stoh*

... a doctor, first aid
... un dottore, il pronto soccorso
... *oon doht-**toh**-reh, eel **prohn**-toh sohk-**kohr**-soh*

May I see ...?
Posso vedere ...?
***pohs**-soh veh-**deh**-reh ...*

... your insurance certificate
... la sua assicurazione
... *lah **soo**-ah ahs-see-koo-raht-see-**oh**-neh*

Contact the ... company
Contatti la compagnia ...
*kohn-**taht**-tee lah kohm-pahn-**yee**-ah ...*

... insurance ...
... di assicurazione
*...dee ahs-see-koo-raht-see-**oh**-neh*

I want a copy ...
Vorrei una copia ...
*vohr-**reh**-ee **oo**-nah **koh**-pee-ah ...*

... of the police report
... del rapporto di polizia
... *dehl rahp-**pohr**-toh dee poh-leet-**see**-ah*

Where is the ... consulate?
Dov'è il consolato ...?
*doh-**veh** eel kohn-soh-**lah**-toh ...*

... American, Australian ...
... Americano, Australiano ...
... *ah-meh-ree-**kah**-noh, ou-stah-lee-**ah**-noh*

... British, Canadian ...
... Britannico, Canadese ...
*... bree-**tahn**-nee-koh, cah-nah-**deh**-seh ...*

... Irish, New Zealand
... Irlandese, Neozelandese
*... eer-lahn-**deh**-seh, neh-oh-tseh-lahn-**deh**-seh*

Are you willing to be a witness?
Vorrebbe testimoniare?
*vohr-**rehb**-beh teh-stee-moh-nee-**ah**-reh*

Your name ... please
Il suo nome ... per favore
*eel **soo**-oh **noh**-meh ... pehr fah-**voh**-reh*

... and address ...
... e l'indirizzo ...
*... eh leen-dee-**reet**-soh ...*

(He), she ... has hurt (his) her head ...
(Lui), lei ... ha battuto la testa ...
*(**loo**-ee), **leh**-ee ah baht-**too**-toh lah **teh**-stah*

... is badly injured
... è seriamente ferito/a
*... **eh** seh-ree-ah-**mehn**-teh feh-**ree**-toh/ah*

... losing blood, unconscious
... perde sangue, è inconscio/a
*pehr-deh **sahn**-gweh, **eh** een-**kohn**-shoh/ah*

He (she) has been stung by a ...
È stato(a) punto(a) da una ...
*eh stah-toh (-tah) **poon**-toh(-ah) dah **oo**-nah*

... bee, scorpion, wasp
... ape, scorpione, vespa
*... **ah**-peh, skohr-pee-**oh**-neh, **veh**-spah*

I've been bitten ...
Sono stato morso ...
*soh-noh **stah**-toh **mohr**-soh ...*

He (she) has been bitten ...
È stato(a) morso ...
*eh stah-toh(-tah) **mohr**-soh ...*

... by a (dog), insect
... da un (cane), insetto
*... dah oon (**kah**-neh), een-**seht**-toh*

I have something in my eye
Ho qualcosa nell'occhio
*oh kwahl-**koh**-zah nehl-**lohk**-kee-oh*

I must see a dentist ...
Ho bisogno di un dentista ...
*oh bee-**zohn**-yoh dee oon dehn-**tee**-stah ...*

... as soon as possible
... al più presto
*... ahl pee-**oo preh**-stoh*

Can you give me ...
Potrebbe fissarmi ...
*poh-**trehb**-beh fees-**sahr**-mee ...*

... an appointment for ... *(see pages 15-20)*
... un appuntamento per ...
*... oon ahp-poon-tah-**mehn**-toh ...*

No sooner than that?
Non prima di così?
*nohn **pree**-mah dee koh-**zee***

This tooth hurts
Questo dente mi fa male
***kweh**-stoh **dehn**-teh mee fah **mah**-leh*

I've lost a filling
Ho perso un'otturazione
*oh **pehr**-soh oo-noht-too-raht-see-**oh**-neh*

I have broken / chipped ...
Ho rotto un dente ...
*oh **roht**-toh oon **dehn**-teh ...*

... my dentures
... la mia dentiera
*... lah **mee**-ah dehn-tee-**eh**-rah*

... this tooth
... questo dente
*... **kweh**-stoh **dehn**-teh*

Can you fill it?
Potrebbe otturarlo?
*poh-**trehb**-beh oht-too-**rahr**-loh*

I do not want the tooth out
Non voglio togliere il dente
*nohn **vohl**-yoh **tohl**-yeh-reh eel **dehn**-teh*

Can you fix it ...?
Potrebbe sistemarlo ...?
*poh-**trehb**-beh see-steh-**mahr**-loh ...*

... (temporarily), now
... (provvisoriamente), ora
*... (prohv-vee-sohr-ee-ah-**mehn**-teh), **oh**-rah*

vohl-yoh fah-reh oo-nah rah-dee-oh-grah-fee-ah
Voglio fare una radiografia ...
I will X-ray ...

... deh-ee soo-oh-ee dehn-tee
... dei suoi denti
... your teeth

leh-ee ah oon ah-shehs-soh
Lei ha un ascesso
You have an abscess

deh-voh tohl-yeh-reh eel dehn-teh
Devo togliere il dente
This tooth must come out

Could you give me ... (an anaesthetic) ...?
Potrebbe darmi ... (un anestetico) ...?
poh-trehb-beh dahr-mee (oon ah-neh-steh-tee-koh)

.. an injection ... first
.. un'iniezione ... prima
.. oon-een-ee-eht-see-oh-neh ... pree-mah

see shah-kwee lah bohk-kah, pehr fah-voh-reh
Si sciacqui la bocca, per favore
Please rinse out your mouth

Can you recommend ...?
Potrebbe raccomandarmi ...?
*poh-**trehb**-beh rahk-koh-mahn-**dahr**-mee ...*

Please call ...
Per favore, chiami ...
*pehr fah-**voh**-reh, kee-**ah**-mee ...*

... a doctor
... un dottore
*... oon doht-**toh**-reh*

I have difficulty breathing. I have ...
Faccio fatica a respirare. Ho ...
***fahch**-choh fah-**tee**-kah ah reh-spee-**rah**-reh. oh*

... diarrhoea, palpitations
... la diarrea, palpitazioni
*lah dee-ahr-**reh**-ah, pahl-pee-tah-tsee-**oh**-nee*

... a pain in my chest
... un dolore al petto
*... oon doh-**loh**-reh ahl **peht**-toh*

... sunstroke, I feel dizzy
... un colpo di sole, mi gira la testa
*oon **kohl**-poh dee **soh**-leh, mee **jee**-rah lah **teh**-stah*

I'm constipated
Sono constipato
*soh-noh kohn-stee-**pah**-toh*

I can't (eat) ...
non posso (mangiare) ...
*nohn **pohs**-soh (mahn-**jah**-reh) ...*

.. sleep, breathe
.. dormire, respirare
*.. dohr-**mee**-reh, reh-spee-**rah**-reh*

.. keeps bleeding
Continuo a sanguinare ...
*cohn-**tee**-noo-oh ah sahn-gwee-**nah**-reh ...*

My nose ...
.. dal naso
*.. dahl **nah**-zoh*

I'm (a diabetic)
Sono (diabetico)
*soh-noh (dee-ah-**beh**-tee-koh)*

.. allergic to penicillin
.. allergico alla penicillina
*ahl-**lehr**-jee-koh **ahl**-lah peh-nee-cheel-**lee**-nah*

This is my ...
Questa è la mia ...
kweh-stah eh la mee-ah ...

... usual medicine
... medicina abituale
... *meh-dee-chee-nah ah-bee-too-ah-leh*

My blood pressure ...
La mia pressione sanguinea ...
lah mee-ah prehs-see-oh-neh sahn-gwee-nee-ah

... is too high (low)
... è troppo alta (bassa)
... *eh trohp-poh ahl-tah (bahs-sah)*

I had a heart attack (stroke) ...
Ho avuto un infarto (un colpo) ...
oh ah-voo-toh oon een-far-toh (oon kohl-poh)

... years (months) ago
... anni (mesi) fa
... *ahn-nee (meh-zee) fah*

I'm / she is ... months pregnant
Sono / lei è incinta di ... mesi
soh-noh/leh-ee eh een-cheen-tah dee ... meh-zee

Italy has two police corps, the *polizia (poh-lee-**tsee**-ah)* and *carabinieri (kah-rah-bee-nee-**eh**-ree)*. In an emergency you can phone either of them (polizia 113, carabinieri 112). They can also arrange for an ambulance. Otherwise it is best to go personally to the STAZIONE DI POLIZIA or STAZIONE DEI CARABINIERI and explain yourself there.

STOP THIEF!
FERMATE IL LADRO!
*fehr-**mah**-teh eel **lahd**-roh!*

Call the police!
Chiamate la polizia!
*kee-ah-**mah**-teh lah poh-leet-**see**-ah*

Where's the (main) ...?
Dov'è la (principale) ...?
*doh-**veh** lah (preen-chee-**pah**-leh) ...*

... police station
... stazione di polizia
*... staht-see-**oh**-neh dee poh-leet-**see**-ah*

I want to report a theft ...
Vorrei denunciare un furto ...
*vohr-**reh**-ee deh-noon-**chah**-reh oon **foor**-toh*

... my ... has been stolen
... il mio ... è stato rubato
*... eel **mee**-oh ... eh **stah**-toh roo-**bah**-toh*

... (money), pounds, dollars ...
... (denaro), sterline, dollari ...
*... (deh-**nah**-roh), stehr-**lee**-neh, **dohl**-lah-ree*

... credit cards ...
... carte di credito ...
*... **kahr**-teh dee **kreh**-dee-toh ...*

... Eurocheques, travellers' cheques ...
... Eurocheques, travellers' cheques ...
*... eh-**oo**-roh-shehks, **trah**-veh-ler shehks ...*

I've lost ... (my handbag)
Ho perso ... (la mia borsa)
*oh **pehr**-soh ... (lah **mee**-ah **bohr**-sah)*

... my wallet
... il mio portafogli
*... eel **mee**-oh pohr-tah-**fohl**-yee*

... passport, luggage
... passaporto, bagaglio
... *pahs-sah-**pohr**-toh, bah-**gahl**-yoh*

I would like to report the theft ...
Vorrei denunciare il furto ...
*vohr-**reh**-ee deh-noon-**chah**-reh eel **foor**-toh*

... of my car ...
... della mia automobile ...
... ***dehl**-lah **mee**-ah ou-toh-**moh**-bee-leh ...*

... the registration number is ...
... il numero di targa è ...
... *eel **noo**-meh-roh dee **tahr**-gah eh ...*

... of ... colour ... *(see pages 151-152)*
... di colore ...
... *dee koh-**loh**-reh ...*

It was stolen from ... street ...
È stata rubata in via ...
***eh stah**-tah roo-**bah**-tah een **vee**-ah ...*

... near to ...
... vicino a ...
... *vee-**chee**-noh ah ...*

... this morning, yesterday evening
... questa mattina, ieri sera
... *kweh-stah maht-tee-nah, ee-eh-ree seh-rah*

... this afternoon, yesterday night
... questo pomeriggio, ieri notte
kweh-stoh poh-meh-reej-joh, ee-eh-ree noht-teh

I would like to report the snatching ...
Vorrei denunciare lo scippo ...
vohr-reh-ee deh-noon-chah-reh loh sheep-poh ...

... of my ... (suitcase) ...
... della mia ... (valigia) ...
... *dehl-lah mee-ah ... (vah-lee-jah) ...*

... camera ...
... macchina fotografica ...
...*mahk-kee-nah foh-toh-grah-fee-kah ...*

... of my (watch), wallet
... del mio (orologio), portafoglio
... *dehl mee-oh oh-roh-loh-joh, pohr-tah-fohl-yoh*

... of my passport
... del mio passaporto
... *dehl mee-oh pahs-sah-pohr-toh*

... of my driving licence
... della mia patente di guida
*dehl-lah **mee**-ah pah-**tehn**-teh dee **gwee**-dah*

One thug on foot ...
Un energumeno a piedi ...
*oon ehn-ehr-**goo**-meh-noh ah pee-**eh**-dee ...*

... two on a motorcycle
... due in motocicletta
*... **doo**-eh een moh-toh-cheek-**leht**-tah*

... a man, a woman
... un uomo, una donna
*... oon **woh**-moh, **oo**-nah **dohn**-nah*

... a lady, a young boy
... una signora, un ragazzetto
*... **oo**-na see-ny-**oh**-rah, oon rah-gaht-**seht**-toh*

... a young man in his twenties
... un giovanotto sui vent'anni
*oon joh-vah-**noht**-toh **soo**-ee vehn-**tahn**-nee*

... an elegant gentleman
... un signore distinto
*... oon seen-**yoh**-reh dee-**steen**-toh*

I'd like to have breakfast
Vorrei fare colazione
*vohr-**reh**-ee **fah**-reh koh-laht-see-**oh**-neh*

I want (orange) juice ...
Vorrei del succo (d'arancia) ...
*vohr-**reh**-ee dehl **soo**-koh (dah-**rahn**-chah)*

... grapefruit, tomato ...
... di pompelmo, di pomodoro ...
*... dee pohm-**pehl**-moh, dee poh-moh-**doh**-roh*

... (small black) coffee ...
... del caffè (ristretto nero) ...
*... dehl kahf-**feh** (ree-**streht**-toh **neh**-roh) ...*

... decaffeinated, white
... decaffeinato, con latte
*... deh-kahf-feh-ee-**nah**-toh, kohn **laht**-teh*

... tea with (milk), lemon ...
... del tè con (latte), limone ...
*... dehl **teh** kohn (**laht**-teh), lee-**moh**-neh ...*

... cream, sugar
... panna, zucchero
*... **pahn**-nah, **tsoo**-keh-roh*

... **bacon and eggs** ...
... delle uova con la pancetta ...
... *dehl*-leh **woh**-vah kohn lah pahn-**cheht**-tah

... **some eggs** ... (fried), soft-boiled ...
... delle uova ... (fritte), sode ...
... *dehl*-leh **woh**-vah ... (**freet**-teh), **soh**-deh ...

... **scrambled** ...
... strapazzate ...
... strah-paht-**sah**-teh ...

... **some bread, toast** ...
... del pane, dei tost ...
... dehl **pah**-neh, **deh**-ee tohst ...

... **rolls, butter** ...
... delle rosette, del burro ...
... *dehl*-leh roh-**zeht**-teh, dehl **boor**-roh ...

... **honey** ...
... del miele ...
... dehl mee-**eh**-leh ...

... **jam (marmalade)** (literally, orange jam)
... della marmellata (d'arance)
dehl-lah mahr-mehl-**lah**-tah (dah-**rahn**-cheh)

Give me one of those ...
Mi dia uno di quelli ...
*mee **dee**-ah **oo**-noh dee **kwehl**-lee ...*

... to the left (right)
... a sinistra (destra)
*... ah see-**nee**-strah (**deh**-strah)*

... above, below, please
... sopra, sotto, per favore
*... **soh**-prah, **soht**-toh, pehr fah-**voh**-reh*

It's to take away
È da portare via
*eh dah pohr-**tah**-reh **vee**-ah*

... a sandwich with (cheese)
... un panino col (formaggio)
*... oon pah-**nee**-noh kohl (fohr-**maj**-joh)*

... eggs and asparagus
... uova e asparagi
*... **woh**-vah eh ah-**spah**-rah-jee*

... ham, Parma ham
... prosciutto, Prosciutto di Parma
*proh-**shoot**-toh, proh-**shoot**-toh dee **pahr**-mah*

... **Russian salad, tuna**
... insalata russa, tonno
... *een-sah-**lah**-tah **roos**-sah, **tohn**-noh*

... **salami, sausages**
... salame, salsiccia
... *sah-**lah**-meh, sahl-**seech**-chah*

... **a soft sandwich, a small soft sandwich**
... un tramezzino, una tartina
... *oon trah-med-**zee**-noh, **oo**-nah tahr-**tee**-nah*

... **a small pizza**
... una pizzetta
... *oo-nah peet-**tseht**-tah*

... **a crostino, a toast**
... un crostino, un tost
... *oon kroh-**stee**-noh, oon tohst*

... **a slice of cake, biscuits**
... una fetta di torta, biscotti
... *oo-nah **feht**-tah dee **tohr**-tah, bee-**skoht**-tee*

... **a chocolate bar**
... una tavoletta di cioccolata
*oo-nah tah-voh-**leht**-tah dee chohk-koh-**lah**-tah*

... **fruit pie**
... torta alla frutta
... ***tohr**-tah **ahl**-lah **froo**-tah*

... **meat pie**
... torta salata alla carne
... ***tohr**-tah sah-**lah**-tah **ahl**-lah **kahr**-neh*

... **crisps, chips**
... patatine, patate fritte
... *pah-tah-**tee**-neh, pah-**tah**-teh **free**-teh*

... **pickles, mustard**
... sottoaceti, senape
... *soht-toh-ah-**cheh**-tee, **seh**-nah-peh*

... **hot chocolate**
... cioccolata calda
... *chohk-koh-**lah**-tah **kahl**-dah*

... **soft drink**
... bibita analcolica
... ***bee**-bee-tah ah-nahl-**koh**-lee-kah*

... **lemonade**
... limonata
... *lee-moh-**nah**-tah*

... a glass ... (of white wine)
... un bicchiere ... (di bianco)
... *oon bee-kee-**eh**-reh ... (dee bee-**ahn**-koh)*

... of (house) red wine
... di rosso (della casa)
... *dee **rohs**-soh (**dehl**-lah **kah**-zah)*

... of sparking white wine
... di prosecco / cartizze
... *dee proh-**sehk**-koh / kahr-**teet**-tseh*

... an aperitif
... un aperitivo
... *oon ah-peh-ree-**tee**-voh*

... a tea, a coffee
... un tè, un caffè
... *oon **teh**, oon kahf-**feh***

... a coffee with milk
... un caffè al latte
... *oon kahf-**feh** ahl **laht**-teh*

... a coffee with cognac
... un caffè corretto al cognac
... *oon kahf-**feh** kohr-**reht**-toh ahl kohn-**yahk***

Have you ... a table for ...?
Avrebbe ... un tavolo per ...?
*ah-**vrehb**-beh ... **oon tah**-voh-loh **pehr** ...*

... a quiet table ...
... un tavolo tranquillo ...
*... **oon tah**-voh-loh trahn-**kweel**-loh ...*

... in a non-smoking area ...
... nell'ala per non-fumatori ...
*... nehl-**lah**-la **pehr nohn**-foo-mah-**toh**-ree ...*

... a table near the window ...
... un tavolo vicino alla finestra ...
***oon tah**-voh-loh vee-**chee**-noh **ahl**-lah fee-**neh**-strah*

... one on the terrace, outside
... sulla terrazza, all'aperto
*... **sool**-lah tehr-**rah**-tsah, **ahll** ah-**pehr**-toh*

We are in a hurry
Abbiamo fretta
*ahb-bee-**ah**-moh **freht**-tah*

Please bring me the menu
Mi porti il menù, per favore
***mee poh**-tee **eel** meh-**noo**, **pehr** foh-**voh**-reh*

Prezzo fisso menù (turistico)
preht-tsoh fees-soh meh-noo (too-ree-stee-koh)
Fixed-price (tourist) menu

Il piatto del giorno
eel pee-aht-toh dehl johr-noh
The dish of the day

La specialità della casa
lah speh-chah-lee-tah dehl-lah kah-sah
The speciality of the house

La specialità locale
lah speh-chee-ah-lee-tah loh-kah-leh
The local speciality

Piatti di carne ...
pee-aht-tee dee kahr-neh ...
Meat dishes ...

... con contorni di verdure
... kohn kohn-tohr-nee dee vehr-doo-rah
... accompanied by vegetables

Piatti freddi (caldi)
pee-aht-tee frehd-dee (kahl-dee)
Cold (hot) dishes

191

Verdure a scelta
*vehr-**doo**-reh ah **shel**-tah*
Choice of vegetables

Verdure (frutta) di stagione
*vehr-**doo**-reh (**froo**-tah) dee stah-**joh**-neh*
Vegetables (fruit) in season

Attesa: venti minuti
*aht-**teh**-zah: **vehn**-tee mee-**noo**-tee*
Waiting time 20 minutes

Tariffe supplementari
*tah-**reef**-feh soop-pleh-mehn-**tah**-ree*
Supplementary charges

Pane (grissini) inclusi
***pah**-neh (gree-**see**-nee) een-**kloo**-see*
Bread (grissini) included

Coperto inclusi
*koh-**pehr**-toh een-**kloo**-see*
Cover charge included

Servizio (IVA) incluso
*sehr-**veet**-see-oh (**Ee**-vah) een-**kloo**-zoh*
Service (VAT) included

Under Italian law, all restaurants must issue a bill showing IVA (VAT), which the customer must be able to produce, or face a fine. Normally this also includes cover and service charges.

It is the custom to leave a small tip for the waiter or waitress. This varies from a few hundred lire (in a café or a bar) to a few thousand. Italians generally do not discriminate by the type of establishment, but rather by the kindness and ability of the individual server. It is up to you to decide how much you want to give, depending on your appreciation of the service, or lack of it.

If you wish to exclude certain ingredients, you say: **Per favore, senza aglio** *(garlic)*, **noci di ogni genere** (any sort of nuts), **sale** (salt), **olio di oliva** (olive oil), **burro** (butter), **grassi** (fats).

*Per fah-**voh**-reh, **sehn**-tsah **ahl**-yoh, **noh**-chee dee **ohn**-yee **geh**-neh-reh, **sah**-leh, **ohl**-yoh dee oh-**lee**-vah, **boor**-roh, **grahs**-see*

al forno, alla brace griglia
ahl fohr-noh, ahl-lah brah-cheh greel-yah
baked, barbecued

allo spiedo
ahl-loh spee-eh-doh
spit roasted

arrosto / arrostito, bollito
ahr-roh-stoh / ahr-roh-stee-toh, bohl-lee-toh
roasted, boiled

in casseruola / in umido
een kahs-sehr-woh-lah / een oo-mee-doh
casseroled

cotto a vapore
koht-toh ah vah-poh-reh
steamed

fritto / in padella
freet-toh / een pah-dehl-lah
fried

grigliato / alla griglia
greel-yah-toh / ahl-lah greel-yah
grilled

marinato
*mah-ree-**nah**-toh*
marinated

ripieno, scottato
*ree-pee-**eh**-noh, skoht-**tah**-toh*
stuffed, poached

stufato / cotto in umido
*stoo-**fah**-toh / **koht**-toh een **oo**-mee-doh*
stewed

affumicato, al sangue
*ahf-foo-mee-**kah**-toh, ahl **sahn**-gweh*
smoked, underdone

medio, ben cotto
*__meh__-dee-oh, behn **koht**-toh*
medium done, well done

con (capperi), aglio
*kohn (**kahp**-peh-ree), **ahl**-yoh*
with (capers), garlic

con chiodi di garofano
*kohn kee-**oh**-dee dee gah-**roh**-fah-noh*
with cloves

Antipasti misti
*ahn-tee-**pah**-stee **mee**-stee*
Mixed hors d'oeuvres

Acciughe marinate
*ahch-**choo**-geh mah-ree-**nah**-teh*
Anchovies marinated in lemon juice,
olive oil, garlic, herbs

Cozze ripiene
***koht**-tseh ree-pee-**eh**-neh*
Mussels stuffed with breadcrumbs and
herbs, coated and deep-fried

Crema di cannellini
***kreh**-mah dee kahn-nehl-**lee**-nee*
A cannellini cream flavoured with
porcini mushrooms and herbs

Cuori di carciofo in olio d'oliva
***kwoh**-ree dee kahr-**choh**-foh een **oh**-lyo doh-**lee**-vah*
Artichoke hearts in olive oil

Fiori di zucchini fritti
*fee-**oh**-ree dee tsook-**kee**-nee **free**-tee*
Courgette flowers coated in a batter of
flour and beer, and deep-fried

Insalata di frutti di mare su pane fritto
*een-sah-**lah**-tah dee **froot**-tee dee **mah**-reh*
*soo **pah**-neh **freet**-toh*
Shellfish salad on fried bread

Frutti di mare:
granchi, cozze, ostriche, vongole, molluschi
***grahn**-kee, **koht**-tseh, **oh**-stree-keh,*
***vohn**-goh-leh, mohl-**loo**-skee*
crabs, mussels, oysters, clams, molluscs

Insalata di moscardini
*een-sah-**lah**-tah dee moh-skahr-**dee**-nee*
Baby octopus marinated in lemon juice,
olive oil, garlic and herbs

Prosciutto (di Parma) e melone
*proh-**shoot**-toh (dee **Pahr**-mah) eh meh-**loh**-neh*
Raw smoked pork (Parma ham) and melon

Uova alla fiorentina
***woh**-vah **ahl**-lah fee-oh-rehn-**tee**-nah*
Eggs florentine

Zucchini alla scapece
*tsook-**kee**-nee **ahl**-lah skah-**peh**-cheh*
Marinated courgettes

Brodo di (carne), di pollo
broh-doh dee (kahr-neh), dee pohl-loh
Broth of (meat), chicken

Pasta e fagioli
pah-stah eh fah-joh-lee
Pasta and bean soup

Minestra di legumi
mee-neh-strah dee leh-goo-mee
Soup of pulses: onions, beans, mushrooms and lentils

Tortellini in brodo
tohr-tehl-lee-nee een broh-doh
Meat-filled pasta sachets in chicken broth

Zuppa di pesce piccante, crema di ...
dzoop-pah dee peh-sheh pee-kahn-teh, kreh-mah dee ...
Chowder (spicy seafood stew), cream of ...

Zuppa Pavese (brodo con uova battute e formaggio)
dzoop-pah Pah-veh-zeh (broh-doh kohn woh-vah baht-too-teh eh fohr-maj-joh)
Pavese soup (broth with beaten egg and cheese)

Agnolotti al burro e salvia
ahn-yoh-loht-tee ahl boor-roh eh sahl-vee-ah
Ravioli (large pasta sachets filled with
spinach and ricotta cheese) with a butter
and fresh sage sauce

Bigoli all'anatra (Bigoli col'arna)
*bee-goh-lee ahl-lah-nah-trah (bee-goh-lee
koh-lahr-nah)*
Fresh, thick egg spaghetti cooked in a
duck broth and served with a duck sauce

Gnocchetti sardi al ragù
nyok-keht-tee sahr-dee ahl rah-goo
Sardininan pasta with meat sauce

Gnocchi alla Romana
nyok-kee ahl-lah Roh-mah-nah
Small balls of semolina (bound with egg)
and baked in the oven

Gnocchi di patate
nyok-kee dee pah-tah-teh
Small balls of potato dumpling, boiled in
water and served with Parmesan and
melted butter

Lasagne alla bolognese
lah-zahn-yeh ahl-lah boh-lohn-yeh-zeh
Lasagne with bolognese sauce, white
sauce, and Parmesan cheese

Linguine con aragosta
leen-gwee-neh kohn ah-rah-goh-stah
Fresh egg thin tagliatelle with lobster sauce

Orecchiette al pomodoro
oh-rek-kee-eht-teh ahl poh-moh-doh-roh
Small ear-shaped pasta with tomato sauce

Pasta ai frutti di mare
pah-stah ah-ee froot-tee dee mah-reh
Pasta with tomatoes, olives, garlic,
clams, and mussels

Pasta ai peperoni
pah-stah ah-ee peh-peh-roh-nee
Pasta with tomatoes, red peppers, bacon,
onions, garlic and white wine

Pasta alla bolognese
pah-stah ahl-lah boh-lohn-yeh-zeh
Pasta with a sauce of tomatoes, minced
meat, onions and herbs

Pasta alla carbonara
*pah-stah **ahl**-lah kahr-boh-**nah**-rah*
Pasta with smoked ham, cheese, eggs and olive oil

Pasta alla siciliana
*pah-stah **ahl**-lah see-chee-lee-**ah**-nah*
Pasta with garlic, olive oil, sweet peppers, anchovies, and Parmesan

Pasta fresca al ragù
*pah-stah **freh**-skah ahl rah-**goo***
Various sorts of fresh egg pasta with a meat sauce

Ravioli ai funghi
*rah-vee-**oh**-lee **ah**-ee **foon**-gee*
Large tortellini (ravioli) with a mushroom sauce

Tortelli di zucca
*tohr-**tehl**-lee dee **dzook**-kah*
Pumpkin ravioli

Tortellini alla panna (e salvia)
*tohr-tehl-**lee**-nee **ahl**-lah **pahn**-nah (eh sahl-vee-ah)*
Tortellini with a cream sauce (and sage)

Risi e bisi
*ree-zee eh **bee**-zee*
Risotto with peas and bacon

Riso al burro
*ree-zoh ahl **boor**-roh*
Boiled rice with butter and grated
Parmesan

Riso al pomodoro
*ree-zoh ahl poh-moh-**doh**-roh*
Rice with tomato sauce and grated
Parmesan sauce

Risotto ai funghi
*ree-**zoht**-toh **ah**-ee **foon**-gee*
Mushroom risotto

Risotto alla milanese
*ree-**zoht**-toh **ahl**-lah mee-lah-**neh**-zeh*
Risotto with marrow, white wine,
saffron, and Parmesan

Risotto con gli asparagi
*ree-**zoht**-toh kohn lyee ah-**spah**-rah-jee*
Asparagus risotto

Anguilla fritta
*ahn-**gweel**-lah **freet**-tah*
Fried eel

Baccalà (alla Vicentina)
*bahk-kah-**lah** (**ahl**-lah Vee-chehn-**tee**-nah)*
Dried salted cod, cooked in milk with
onion, garlic, parsley, anchovies and
cinnamon

Calamaretti in umido
*kah-lah-mah-**reht**-tee een **oo**-mee-doh*
Small braised squids

Capesante al burro e limone
*kah-peh-**sahn**-teh ahl **boor**-roh eh lee-**moh**-neh*
Scallops with butter and lemon

Frittura mista
*freet-**too**-rah **mee**-stah*
Mixed small fried fish and shellfish

Pesce spada, ricci di mare e seppie
***peh**-sheh **spah**-dah, **ree**-chee dee **mah**-reh*
*eh **sehp**-pee-eh*
Swordfish, sea-urchins, cuttlefish

Sogliola al burro con contorno di prezzemolo
*sohl-yee-**oh**-lah ahl **boor**-roh kohn*
*kohn-**tohr**-noh dee preht-**tseh**-moh-loh*
Sole, sauté in butter with a parsley garnish

Seppie al nero
***sehp**-pee-eh ahl **neh**-roh*
Cuttlefish in its own sauce

Stocco alla genovese
***stohk**-koh **ahl**-lah jeh-noh-**veh**-zeh*
Stockfish (dried salted cod) stewed with
olive oil, onions, garlic, anchovies, and
herbs

Triglie alle olive
***treel**-yeh **ahl**-leh oh-**lee**-veh*
Red mullet stewed with olive oil, garlic,
olives, tomatoes, and herbs

Triglia (cefalo) rossa al forno
***treel**-yah (**cheh**-fah-loh) **rohs**-sah ahl **fohr**-noh*
Baked red mullet

Trota marinata
***troh**-tah mah-ree-**nah**-tah*
Marinated trout

Anatra all'arancia
*ah-nah-trah ahl-lah-**rahn**-chah*
Roast duck with orange sauce

Arrosto di agnello
*ahr-**roh**-stoh dee ahn-**yehl**-loh*
Roast lamb

Arrosto di capretto ripieno
*ahr-**roh**-stoh dee kah-**preht**-toh ree-pee-**eh**-noh*
Stuffed roast kid

Arrosto di maiale
*ahr-**roh**-stoh dee mah-ee-**ah**-leh*
Roast pork

Arrosto di manzo
*ahr-**roh**-stoh dee **man**-tsoh*
Roast beef

Arrosto di vitello ...
*ahr-**roh**-stoh dee vee-**tehl**-loh ...*
Roast veal ...

... ripieno
*... ree-pee-**eh**-noh*
... stuffed with eggs, sausage, mushrooms

Bistecca alla Fiorentina, con pepe, limone e prezzemolo
*bee-**stehk**-kah **ahl**-lah fee-oh-rehn-**tee**-nah, kohn **peh**-peh, lee-**moh**-neh eh preh-**tseh**-moh-loh*
Grilled steak, with pepper, lemon, parsley seasoning

Braciole ripiene di prosciutto, formaggio e tartufi
*brah-**choh**-leh ree-pee-**eh**-neh dee proh-**shoot**-toh, fohr-**maj**-joh eh tahr-**too**-fee*
Chops stuffed with ham, cheese and truffles

Cinghiale arrosto
*cheen-gee-**ah**-leh ahr-**roh**-stoh*
Roast wild boar

Coniglio alle olive
*koh-**neel**-yoh **ahl**-leh oh-**lee**-veh*
Stewed rabbit with olives

Fagiano al tartufo di Norcia
*fah-**jah**-noh ahl tahr-**too**-foh dee **Nohr**-chah*
Roast pheasant served with a hot sauce of butter and wine and freshly-grated truffles

Fegato alla veneziana
*feh-gah-toh **ahl**-lah veh-ne-tsee-**ah**-nah*
Calves' liver fried with onions, served
with chopped parsley, pepper and lemon

Filetto di capriolo al barolo
*fee-**leht**-toh dee kah-pree-**oh**-loh ahl
bah-**roh**-loh*
Venison fillet marinated and stewed in
Barolo wine

Lepre in salmì
*leh-preh een sahl-**mee***
Hare marinated in wine and herbs and
then fried and further prepared with
other meats

Ossobuco alla milanese
*ohs-soh-**boo**-koh **ahl**-lah mee-lah-**neh**-zeh*
Veal marrowbones stewed in the
Milanese way

Palombo (colombaccio) allo spiedo
*pah-**lohm**-boh (koh-lohm-**bahch**-oh)
ahl-loh spee-**eh**-doh*
Spit-roasted woodpigeon

Petti di pollo alla pizzaiola
peht-tee dee pohl-loh ahl-lah
peet-tsah-ee-oh-lah
Breast of chicken in a tomato and herb
sauce

Pollo alla diavola
pohl-loh ahl-lah dee-ah-voh-lah
Spicy grilled chicken

Polenta e salsicce / (luganeghe)
poh-lehn-tah eh sahl-seech-cheh /
(loo-gah-neh-hee)
Grilled polenta and sausages /(long,
curly, sweetish sausages)

Pollo arrosto / (allo spiedo)
pohl-loh ahr-roh-stoh (ahl-loh spee-eh-doh)
Roast (spit roast) chicken

Porcellino arrosto
pohr-chehl-lee-noh ahr-roh-stoh
Roast sucking pig

Stufato di carne (o pollo)
stoo-fah-toh dee kahr-neh (oh pohl-loh)
Stewed beef (or poultry)

Stufato di coniglio con polenta
stoo-fah-toh dee koh-nee-lee-yoh kohn
poh-lehn-tah
Rabbit stew with maize paste

Stufato di manzo con salsicce di maiale
stoo-fah-toh dee mahn-tsoh kohn
sahl-seech-cheh dee mah-ee-ah-leh
Beef stew with pork sausage

Tacchino arrosto
tahk-kee-noh ahr-roh-stoh
Roast turkey

Vitello tonnato
vee-tehl-loh tohn-nah-toh
Cold veal with tuna sauce, capers and
squeezed fresh lemon

Zampone e lenticchie
dzahm-poh-neh eh lehn-teek-kee-eh
Stuffed pig's trotter and lentils

Zampone ripieno
dzahm-poh-neh ree-pee-eh-noh
Pig's trotter stuffed with pork, boiled, sliced

barbabietole / bietole
*bahr-bah-bee-**eh**-toh-leh / bee-**eh**-toh-leh*
beetroot

Caponata
*kah-poh-**nah**-tah*
Sicilian vegetable stew

carciofi, castagne
*kahr-**choh**-fee, cah-**stahn**-yeh*
artichokes, chestnuts

Carciofi in agrodolce
*kahr-**choh**-fee een ah-groh-**dohl**-cheh*
Artichokes in a sweet-sour sauce

Carcioifi ripieni
*kahr-**choh**-fee ree-pee-**eh**-nee*
Stewed artichokes with a vegetable filling

catalogne, coste
*kahtah-**lohn**-yeh, **koh**-steh*
steamed and fried green leaves (eaten with meat)

cavolfiore, cavolo
*kah-vohl-fee-**oh**-reh, **kah**-voh-loh*
cauliflower, cabbage

cavolini di Bruxells, ceci
*kah-voh-**lee**-nee dee Brook-**sehls**, **cheh**-chee*
Brussels sprouts, chick-peas

Cavolo ripieno
***kah**-voh-loh ree-pee-**eh**-noh*
Savoy cabbage parcels with mixed meat filling

cavolo verde, cavolo nero
***kah**-voh-loh **vehr**-deh, **kah**-voh-loh **neh**-roh*
green cabbage, black cabbage

cetrioli, cicoria, capperi
*cheh-tree-**oh**-lee, chee-koh-**ree**-ah, **kahp**-peh-ree*
cucumbers, chicory, capers

cipolle, cipolline, cren
*chee-**pohl**-leh, chee-pohl-**lee**-nee, krehn*
onions, shallots, horseradish

fagiolini, fagioloni, fave
*fah-joh-**lee**-nee, fah-joh-**lee**-nee, **fah**-veh*
french beans, haricot beans, broad beans

finocchi, funghi, indivia
*fee-**nok**-kee, **foon**-gee, een-**dee**-vee-ah*
fennel, mushrooms, endive

Fiori di zucchini ripieni
*fee-**oh**-ree dee dzook-**kee**-nee ree-pee-**eh**-nee*
Stuffed and deep-fried courgette flowers

insalata (mista) verde
*een-sah-**lah**-tah (**mee**-stah) **vehr**-deh*
(mixed) green salad

lattuga, lenticchie, melanzane
*laht-**too**-gah, lehn-**tee**-kee-eh, meh-lahn-**tsah**-neh*
lettuce, lentils, aubergines

Melanzane fritte
*meh-lahn-**tsah**-neh **freet**-teh*
Deep-fried aubergines

Peperoni e olive
*peh-peh-**roh**-nee eh oh-**lee**-veh*
Shallow-fried peppers and olives

Peperoni fritti
*peh-peh-**roh**-nee **freet**-tee*
Fried peppers

Peperoni ripieni
*peh-peh-**roh**-nee ree-pee-**eh**-nee*
Baked peppers stuffed with vegetables

pomidori, patate, peperoni
*poh-mee-**doh**-ree, pah-**tah**-teh, peh-peh-**roh**-nee*
tomatoes, potatoes, peppers

piselli, porri, radicchio
*pee-**zehl**-lee, **pohr**-ree, rah-**deek**-kee-oh*
potatoes, leeks, chicory

radicchio rosso, ravanelli
*rah-**deek**-kee-oh **rohs**-soh, rah-vah-**nehl**-lee*
bitter red leaves, radish

rape, sedano, spinaci
*rah-peh, **seh**-dah-noh, spee-**nah**-chee*
turnips, celery, spinach

tartufo, zucca, zucchini
*tahr-**too**-foh, **dzook**-kah, dzoo-**kee**-nee*
truffle, pumpkin, courgettes

Uova al tartufo
*woh-vah ahl tahr-**too**-foh*
Oven-baked eggs with truffles

verdure assortite
*vehr-**doo**-reh ahs-sohr-**tee**-teh*
assorted vegetables

aglio, chiodo di garofano
*ahl-yoh, **kee**-oh-doh dee gah-**roh**-fah-noh*
garlic, clove

alloro, basilico, cannella
*ahl-**loh**-roh, bah-**zee**-lee-koh, kahn-**nehl**-lah*
bay-leaves, basil, cinnamon

erba cipollina, cumino
***ehr**-bah chee-pohl-**lee**-nah, koo-**mee**-noh*
chives, cumin

maggiorana / origano, menta
*mahj-joh-**rah**-nah / oh-**ree**-gah-noh, **mehn**-tah*
marjoram, mint

noce moscata, prezzemolo
***noh**-cheh moh-**skah**-tah, preht-**seh**-moh-loh*
nutmeg, parsley

rosmarino, salvia, timo
*rohz-mah-**ree**-noh, **sahl**-vee-ah, **tee**-moh*
rosemary, sage, thyme

zafferano, zenzero
*dzahf-feh-**rah**-noh, **zdehn**-dzeh-roh*
saffron, ginger

Torte e dolci
tohr-teh eh dohl-chee
Cakes and sweets

Crema di nocciole con panna montata
kreh-mah dee nohch-choh-leh kohn
pahn-nah mohn-tah-tah
Purée of chestnuts with whipped cream

Ricotta con Maraschino
ree-koht-tah kohn Mah-rah-skee-noh
Curd cheese with cherry liqueur

Tartufi di cioccolata
tah-too-fee dee chok-koh-lah-tah
Chocolate truffles

Tiramisù
tee-rah-mee-soo
Soft cake made with Savoyard biscuits,
coffee, eggs, and rum

Zabaglione gelato
tsah-bahl-yoh-neh jeh-lah-toh
Zabaglione icecream (a cream of egg
yolks, sugar, and Marsala wine)

Asiago
*ah-zee-**ah**-goh*
firm, slightly sweet cheese

Caciocavallo
*kah-cho-kah-**vahl**-loh*
firm, ripened horse cheese

Gorgonzola
*gohr-gohn-**tsoh**-lah*
rich, tangy, blue-veined cheese

Mascarpone
*mah-skahr-**poh**-neh*
smooth, delicate, creamy cheese

Mozzarella
*moht-tsah-**rehl**-lah*
soft unripened cheese, often partners tomatoes

Parmigiano
*pahr-mee-**jah**-noh*
very ripened, strong cheese

Pecorino
*peh-koh-**ree**-noh*
hard cheese made from sheeps' milk

albicocche
*ahl-bee-**kohk**-keh*
apricots

arance
*ah-**rahn**-che*
oranges

banana
*bah-**nah**-nah*
banana

ciliegie
*chee-lee-**eh**-jeh*
cherries

fichi
fee-kee
figs

fragole
frah-goh-leh
strawberries

lamponi
*lahm-**poh**-nee*
raspberries

mele
meh-leh
apples

melone
*meh-**loh**-neh*
melon

mirtilli
*meer-**teel**-lee*
blueberries

pere
peh-reh
pears

pesche
peh-skeh
peaches

ribes rosso
ree-behs rohs-soh
redcurrants

ribes nero
ree-behs neh-roh
blackcurrants

Gelati *(jeh-lah-tee)*

Every Italian Gelateria has its own recipes, and it is impossible to list them all here. However, there are a few classics and a variety of *gusti*, the basic ice-cream flavours and ingredients which we list in alphabetical order below, in addition to the fruit flavours, for which please see the previous page.

Caffè *(kahf-feh)* coffee
Cioccolata *(chohk-koh-lah-tah)* chocolate
Dolcelatte *(dohl-cheh-laht-teh)* cream
Malaga *(mah-lah-gah)* cream with raisins and liqueur
Nocciola *(noh-choh-lah)* hazelnut
Panna montata *(pahn-nah mohn-tah-tah)* whipped cream
Pistacchio *(pee-stahk-kee-oh)* pistachio
Stracciatella *(strah-chah-tehl-lah)* cream with pieces of black, bitter chocolate
Vaniglia *(vah-neel-yah)* vanilla

What's on at ... (the cinema)?
Che cosa c'è ... (al cinema)?
*keh **koh**-sah **cheh** ... (ahl **chee**-neh-mah)*

... the theatre, ballet, concert
... al teatro, balletto, concerto
*ahl teh-**ah**-troh, bahl-**leht**-toh, kohn-**chehr**-toh*

... oper(a), -etta, the nightclub
... all'opera, -etta, nightclub
*ahll-**oh**-peh-(rah), -**reht**-tah, ahl **nah**-eet klahb*

At what time does it start?
A che ora comincia?
*ah keh **oh**-rah koh-**meen**-chah*

How much are ...? I'd like ...
Quanto costano ...? Vorrei ...
***kwhan**-toh **koh**-stah-noh ...? vohr-**reh**-ee ...*

... the seats?
... i posti a sedere?
*... ee **poh**-stee ah seh-**deh**-reh*

... a programme, please
... un programma, per favore
*... oon proh-**grahm**-mah, pehr fah-**voh**-reh*

Do you mind if I smoke?
Le dispiace se fumo?
*leh dee-spee-**ah**-cheh seh **foo**-moh*

Do you sell English (cigarettes)?
Vendete sigarette Inglesi?
*vehn-**deh**-teh see-gah-**reht**-teh Een-**gleh**-zee*

... cigars, pipe tobacco
... sigari, tabacco da pipa
*... see-**gah**-ree, tah-**bahk**-koh dah **pee**-pah*

I'd like (a packet) of ...
Vorrei (un pacchetto) di ...
*vohr-**reh**-ee (oon pahk-**keht**-toh) dee ...*

... (filter-tipped), without filters
... con filtro, senza filtro
*... kohn **feel**-troh, **sehn**-tsah **feel**-troh*

... mild, strong
... leggere, forti
*... lehj-**jeh**-reh, **fohr**-tee*

... menthol, king-sized
... al mentolo, lunghe
*... ahl **mehn**-tohl-loh, **loon**-geh*

... matches
... fiammiferi
... *fee-ahm-**mee**-feh-ree*

... lighter fluid
... fluido combustibile da accendino
... ***floo**-ee-doh kohm-boo-**stee**-bee-leh dah
a-chehn-**dee**-noh*

... flints
... pietrine
... *pee-eh-**tree**-neh*

... gas refill ...
... un ricambio ...
... *oon ree-**kahm**-bee-oh ...*

... for this lighter
... per questo accendino
... *pehr **kweh**-stoh ah-chehn-**dee**-noh*

VIETATO FUMARE
No smoking

Where's the nearest ...?
Dov'è il più vicino ...?
*doh-**veh** eel pee-**oo** vee-**chee**-noh ...*

... tennis court
... campo da tennis
... ***kahm**-poh dah **tehn**-nees*

... golf course
... il campo da golf
... *eel **kahm**-poh dah gohlf*

... place to go swimming (fishing)
... posto per nuotare (pescare)
***poh**-stoħ pehr nwoh-**tah**-reh (peh-**skah**-reh)*

... riding school
... maneggio
... *mah-**nehj**-joh*

... water ski facilities
... impianto per sci nautico
... *eem-pee-**ahn**-toh pehr shee **nou**-tee-koh*

What's the cost ...
Quanto costa ...
***kwahn**-toh **koh**-stah ...*

... per hour, round
... per un'ora, per un giro
*... pehr oon**oh**-rah, pehr oon **jee**-roh*

... per day
... per un giorno
*... pehr oon **johr**-noh*

Can I hire ... ?
Posso noleggiare ...?
***pohs**-soh noh-lehj-**jah**-reh ...*

... (a racket), clubs
... una racchetta, delle mazze
*... **oo**-nah rahk-**keht**-tah, **dehl**-leh **maht**-tseh*

... rods
... delle canne da pesca
*... **dehl**-leh **kahn**-neh dah **peh**-skah*

Do I need a permit?
C'è bisogno di un permesso?
***cheh** bee-**zohn**-yoh dee oon pehr-**mehs**-soh*

Where can I get one?
Dove posso chiederne uno?
***doh**-veh **pohs**-soh kee-**eh**-dehr-neh **oo**-noh*

I'd like to see ...
Vorrei vedere ...
*vohr-**reh**-ee veh-**deh**-reh ...*

... a football match
... un partita di calcio
*... oon pahr-**tee**-tah dee **kahl**-choh*

Which teams are playing?
Che squadre giocano?
*keh **skwah**-dreh **joh**-kah-noh*

What's the entrance fee?
Quanto costa l'entrata?
***kwahn**-toh **koh**-stah lehn-**trah**-tah*

Can you get me a ticket?
Può prendermi un biglietto?
***pwoh prehn**-dehr-mee oon beel-**yeht**-toh*

Where's the race track (stadium) for ...?
Dov'è lo stadio per ...?
*doh-**veh** loh **stah**-dee-oh pehr ...*

... car racing
... una gara automobilistica
*... **oo**-nah **gah**-rah ou-toh-moh-bee-**lee**-stee-kah*

On the beach you might see a blue flag, indicating that it is all right to bathe. However, if you should see a red flag, this means that the sea is too rough to bathe, and generally that there is no lifeguard service because of this! The lifeguard is called the bagnino (*bahn-yee-noh*).

Where are the best beaches?
Dove sono le migliori spiagge?
*doh-veh **soh**-noh leh meel-**yoh**-ree spee-**ahj**-jee*

Is there a quiet beach ...?
C'è una spiaggia tranquilla ...?
*cheh oo-nah spee-**ahj**-jah trahn-**kweel**-lah*

... near here. Is it safe?
... qui vicino. È sicuro?
*... kwee vee-**chee**-noh. **eh** see-**koo**-roh*

Can one swim in the sea?
Si può nuotare nel mare?
*see **pwoh** nwoh-**tah**-reh nehl **mah**-reh*

Are there any dangerous currents?
Ci sono correnti pericolose?
chee **soh**-*noh cohr*-**rehn**-*tee peh-ree-koh-**loh**-zee*

Is there a lifeguard?
C'è un bagnino?
cheh *oon bahn-**yee**-noh*

There are some big waves
Ci sono delle grosse onde
chee **soh**-*noh* **dehl**-*leh* **grohs**-*seh* **ohn**-*deh*

Can we water-ski here?
Si può fare sci nautico?
see **pwoh fah**-*reh shee* **nou**-*tee-koh*

We want to go fishing
Vorremmo andare a pescare
vohr-**rehm**-*moh ahn*-**dah**-*reh ah peh*-**skah**-*reh*

Can I hire ... (a boat)?
Si può noleggiare ... (una barca)?
see **pwoh** *noh-lej*-**jah**-*reh (***oo***-nah* **bahr**-*kah)*

... cabin, sunshade
... una cabina, ombrellone
... **oo**-*nah kah*-**bee**-*nah, ohm-brehl*-**loh**-*neh*

... **deckchair**
... sedia a sdraio
... *seh-dee-ah ah zdrah-ee-oh*

... **motor boat**
... una barca a motore
... *oo-nah bahr-kah ah moh-toh-reh*

... **surfboard, water skis**
... un surf a vela, sci d'acqua
... *oon soorf ah veh-lah, shee dahk-kwah*

È PROIBITO BAGNARSI
bathing prohibited

È PROIBITO IMMERGERSI
diving prohibited

PERICOLO
danger

SPIAGGIA PRIVATA
private beach

CORRENTE FORTE
strong current

Is there a swimming pool ...
C'è una piscina ...
cheh **oo**-*nah pee*-**shee**-*nah* ...

Is it open-air, indoor?
È all'aria aperta, al coperto?
eh ahl-**lah**-*ree-ah ah*-**pehr**-*tah, ahl koh*-**pehr**-*toh*

Is it deep? Are there showers?
È profondo? Ci sono docce?
eh proh-**fohn**-*doh? chee* **soh**-*noh* **dohch**-*cheh*

I'd like to hire ... (*see previous pages*)
Vorrei noleggiare ...
vohr-**reh**-*ee noh-lehd*-**jah**-*reh*

What is the hourly rate ...?
Quant'è la retta oraria ... ?
kwahn-**teh** *lah* **reht**-*tah oh*-**rah**-*ree-ah* ...

... (for diving), for surfing
... (per immersioni), surfing
... (pehr eem-mer-see-**oh**-*nee), surfing*

... swimming, children
... per nuotare, per i bambini
... pehr nwoh-**tah**-*reh, pehr ee bahm*-**bee**-*nee*

Where's the nearest ...?
Dov'è la più vicina ...?
*doh-**veh** lah pee-**oo** vee-**chee**-nah*

Is there a ... (ski run) for ...?
C'è una ... (piste da sci) per ...?
***cheh oo**-nah (pee-**steh** dah shee) pehr ...*

... beginners
... principianti
*... preen-chee-pee-**ahn**-tee*

Are there any ski lifts?
Ci sono degli ski-lifts?
*chee **soh**-noh **dehl**-yee ski-lifts*

Can I hire some ... here?
Posso noleggiare delle ... qui?
***pohs**-soh noh-lehj-**jah**-reh **dehl**-leh ... kwee*

... skiing equipment
... un equipaggiamento da sci
*... oon eh-kwee-pahj-jah-**mehn**-toh dah shee*

Can I take lessons ...?
Posso ricevere delle lezioni ...?
***pohs**-soh ree-**cheh**-veh-reh leh-tsee-**oh**-nee*

Do you have ... beer?
Avete una birra ...?
*ah-**veh**-teh **oo**-nah **beer**-rah ...*

I'd like a ... (local) beer
Vorrei ... una birra (locale)
*vohr-**reh**-ee ... **oo**-nah **beer**-rah (loh-**kah**-leh)*

... imported
... d'importazione
*... deem-pohr-tah-tsee-**oh**-neh*

... draught, light, dark
... alla spina, leggera, scura
*... **ahl**-lah **spee**-nah, lehj-**jeh**-rah, **skoo**-rah*

... alcohol-free, low-alcohol
... analcolica, poco alcolica
*ahn-ahl-**koh**-lee-kah, **poh**-koh ahl-**koh**-lee-kah*

I would like a ... please!
Vorrei una ... per favore!
*vohr-**reh**-ee **oo**-nah ... per fah-**voh**-reh*

... not too cold beer ...
... non troppo fredda birra ...
*... nohn **trohp**-poh **frehd**-dah **beer**-rah ...*

Please bring me ...
Per favore, mi porti ...
*pehr fah-**voh**-reh, mee **pohr**-tee ...*

... the wine list
... la lista dei vini
... ***lee**-stah **deh**-ee **vee**-nee*

... a glass of ...
... un bicchiere di ...
... *oon beek-kee-**eh**-reh dee ...*

... a (half) bottle of ...
... una (mezza) bottiglia di ...
... *oo-nah (**mehd**-zah) boht-**teel**-yah dee ...*

... house wine
... vino della casa
... ***vee**-noh **dehl**-lah **kah**-zah*

... red, white, sparkling
... rosso, bianco, frizzante
... ***rohs**-soh, bee-**ahn**-koh, freet-**tsahn**-teh*

Are there any local specialities?
Avete delle specialità locali?
*ah-**veh**-teh **dehl**-leh speh-chah-lee-**tah** loh-**kah**-lee*

Glass, bottle, double
Bicchiere, bottiglia, doppio
*beek-kee-**eh**-reh, boht-**teel**-yah, **dohp**-pee-ah*

Neat, with ... (ice), lemon
Schietto, con ... (ghiaccio), limone
*skee-**eht**-toh, kohn gee-**ahch**-choh, lee-**moh**-neh*

With (seltzer) mineral water
Con (selz) acqua minerale
*kohn (sehlts) **ak**-kwah mee-neh-**rah**-leh*

Amaretto
*ah-mah-**reht**-toh*
bitter almond liqueur

Amaro
*ah-**mah**-roh*
bitter herb liqueur

Anisetta
*ah-nee-**seht**-tah*
aniseed liqueur

Aperitivo
*ah-peh-ree-**tee**-voh*
appetiser wine

Campari
*kahm-**pah**-ree*
branded aperitif

Cinzano
*cheen-**tsah**-noh*
Piedmontese
family producers of
a range of aperitifs
and wines

Genepy
*jehn-eh-**pee***
herb liqueur from
the Aosta Valley

grappa / acqua vite
grahp-pah, *ah*-kwah
vee-teh
spirit distilled from
grape pressings in
the Veneto region

Maraschino
mah-rah-skee-noh
cherry liqueur

Marsala
mahr-sah-lah
sweet, aged Sicilian
wine

Martini
mahr-tee-nee
the Piedmontese
family who
launched the
famous aperitif

Nocino
noh-chee-noh
Modenese nut
liqueur

Rosolio
roh-zoh-lee-oh
sweet, old-fashioned
'ladies' liqueur

Saba, Sapa, Vino Cotto
sah-bah, *sah*-pah,
vee-noh *koht*-toh
evaporated wine
used in cooking

Sambuca
sahm-boo-kah
aniseed liqueur

Slivovitz
slee-voh-veets
Friulian fruit spirit

Strega
streh-gah
herb liqueur

Vino Chinato
vee-noh kee-*nah*-toh
Piedmontese
aperitif

THE SEASONS

spring
la primavera
*lah pree-mah-**veh**-rah*

autumn
l'autunno
*lou-**toon**-noh*

summer
l'estate
*leh-**stah**-teh*

winter
l'inverno
*leen-**vehr**-noh*

FRACTIONS AND PERCENTAGES

three quarters
tre quarti
*treh **kwahr**-tee*

50%
cinquanta per cento
*cheen-**kwahn**-tah
pehr **chehn**-toh*

two-thirds
due terzi
***doo**-eh **tehr**-tsee*

25%
venticinque per cento
*vehn-tee-**cheen**-kweh
pehr **chehn**-toh*

a half
mezzo
***meh**-tsoh*

10%
dieci per cento
*dee-**eh**-chee pehr
chehn-toh*

a quarter
un quarto
***oon kwahr**-toh*

bad (male / female)
cattivo / cattiva
*kaht-**tee**-voh*
*kaht-**tee**-vah*

big
grande
***grahn**-deh*

cheap
a buon mercato
*ah boo-**ohn***
*mehr-**kah**-toh*

cold (male / female)
freddo / fredda
***frehd**-doh / **frehd**-dah*

expensive
caro (male)
kah-roh
cara (female)
kah-rah

early
presto
***preh**-stoh*

easy
facile
***fah**-chee-leh*

empty (malé / female)
vuoto / vuota
*voo-**oh**-toh / voo-**oh**-tah*

far male (female)
lontano (lontana)
*lohn-**tah**-noh(-nah)*

fast
veloce
*veh-**loh**-cheh*

good (male / female)
buono / buona
*boo-**oh**-noh/boo-**oh**-nah*

heavy
pesante
*peh-**sahn**-teh*

high (male / female)
alto / alta
***ahl**-toh / **ahl**-tah*

hot (male / female)
caldo / calda
kahl-doh / *kahl-dah*

new (male / female)
nuovo / nuova
noo-oh-voh/noo-oh-vah

late
tardi
tahr-dee

old
vecchio
vehk-kee-oh

last male (female)
ultimo (ultima)
ool-tee-moh(-mah)

right (-hand side)
a destra
ah deh-strah

left
sinistra
see-nee-strah

right (just) (m / f)
giusto / giusta
joo-stoh / *joo-stah*

light (male / female)
leggero / leggera
lehj-jeh-roh / *(-rah)*

tall (male / female)
alto / alta
ahl-toh / *ahl-tah*

little (male / female)
piccolo / piccola
peek-koh-loh / *(-lah)*

wrong male (female)
sbagliato (sbagliata)
sbah-ly-ah-toh(-tah)

near male (female)
vicino (vicina)
vee-chee-noh(-nah)

young
giovane
joh-vah-neh

WHERE TO FIND

Know before you go

Phonetics and pronunciation   4
Days and months   6
Dates   8
Public holidays   10
Be polite!   13
Time   15
Greetings and introductions   21
How much and how to pay   24
Counting your money   27
Making it clear   32
Using the phone   34
Spell it out   39

Travel

At the airport   41
Going by boat   45
Car breakdowns   48
Road signs   56
Car hire   60
Catching a bus   64
Going by taxi   73
Underground   76
Customs and passports   80
Finding your way   84

Maps and guides   88
Metric equivalents   91
Petrol stations / garages   92
Going by rail   95
Sightseeing   101
Travel agents   107
Trips and excursions   110

Accommodation

Where to stay   113
Your room – booking in   114
Booking in advance   119
Camping   120
Needs and problems in the room   123
Reception / porter / concierge   126
Room service   129
Self-catering   131
Checking out   134

Banking and Shopping

Changing money   135
A chemist's or a perfumery?   138
At the chemist's   139
In the perfumery   142
Cleaning clothes   146
Buying clothes   149
Clothes sizes   153

Gifts and souvenirs   154
At the hairdresser's   158
Photography   162
Post it!   166

Emergencies

Accidents and injuries   169
At the dentist's   173
At the doctor's   176
Loss and theft   179

Food and Entertainment

Eating out – fast food   184
In the restaurant   190
Menus   191
Ways of cooking   194
Soups and appetisers   196
Pasta   199
Rice   202
The fish course   203
Meat, poultry and game   205
Vegetables and salads   210
Herbs and spices   214
Desserts   215
Cheese   216
Fruit   217
Ice cream   218

Nightlife   219
Smokers' needs   220
Playing sports   222
Watching sports   224
Beaches   225
Water sports   228
Winter sports   229
Beers   230
Wines   231
Aperitifs, spirits and liqueurs   232

Further information

The seasons / Fractions and percentages   234
Common adjectives   235